PRAISE FO...
POP...

"One-third of the way through this book, you'll be begging to hire Sam Horn as your consultant. Halfway through, you'll realize she's teaching you enough to do it yourself. Words matter, every one of them, and this book will revolutionize the way you use them." • Seth Godin, author of *Small Is the New Big*

"Lively, fun, and an inspiring guide to getting heard, getting remembered, and getting results." • Ken Blanchard, coauthor of *The One Minute Manager* and *The Secret*

"Sam Horn is the mom of POP! Her book is dangerous. It is filled with practical methods for making your message outstanding and unforgettable." • Michael J. Gelb, author of *How to Think Like Leonardo DaVinci* and *Discover Your Genius*

"Sam Horn's techniques for coining memorable names and slogans are popping-fresh engaging, easy to apply, and jolly good fun." • Richard Lederer, author of *Word Wizard* and cohost of National Public Radio's "A Way with Words"

"Do you want an interesting elevator intro that motivates people to want to know more about you and your business? Buy this book. It will teach you how to intrigue people in the first sixty seconds of meeting them." • Rick Frishman, President of Planned Television Arts, coauthor of *Networking Magic*

"One of the keys to attracting media coverage is to have intriguing, memorable sound bites that grab the attention of broadcast reporters and producers. This book is filled with specific, innovative ways you can craft pitches that do just that." • Jacqueline Deval, author of *Publicize Your Book!*

"*POP!* is full of ways to come up with creative names and marketing slogans that help your products capture people's interest. Every entrepreneur and inventor needs this." • Todd Walker and Jean Golden, creators and hosts of the "Million Dollar Idea" show

continued . . .

"If you want to know how to compose brands and marketing messages that stop people in their tracks, do yourself a favor and buy this innovative book." • Marilynn Mobley, senior vice president of Edelman

"POP! shows how to create those all-important 'sticky' names, slogans, and brands that stay in your customers' minds." • Dewitt Jones, coauthor of *The Nature of Leadership*

"If you're ready to POP! out of any and every crowd and be remembered, let my friend Sam Horn show you how." • Mark Victor Hansen, cocreator of the #1 *New York Times* bestselling series *Chicken Soup for the Soul*

PRAISE FOR *TONGUE FU!*

"This is a terrific book." • Tony Robbins

"Everyone should read it." • John Gray

PRAISE FOR *TAKE THE BULLY BY THE HORNS*

"The perfect guide on how to avoid negative confrontations and face those who intimidate and manipulate you—without sacrificing your integrity." • Dave Pelzer, author of *A Child Called "It"*

PRAISE FOR *CONZENTRATE*

"Fascinating, thought-provoking, and motivating." • Stephen R. Covey, author of *The 7 Habits of Highly Effective People*

For more comments about Sam Horn's books,
visit www.SamHorn.com

POP!

CREATE THE PERFECT PITCH, TITLE, AND TAGLINE FOR ANYTHING

Sam Horn

A PERIGEE BOOK

A PERIGEE BOOK
Published by the Penguin Group
Penguin Group (USA) Inc.
375 Hudson Street, New York, New York 10014, USA
Penguin Group (Canada), 90 Eglinton Avenue East, Suite 700, Toronto, Ontario M4P 2Y3, Canada
(a division of Pearson Penguin Canada Inc.)
Penguin Books Ltd., 80 Strand, London WC2R 0RL, England
Penguin Group Ireland, 25 St. Stephen's Green, Dublin 2, Ireland (a division of Penguin Books Ltd.)
Penguin Group (Australia), 250 Camberwell Road, Camberwell, Victoria 3124, Australia
(a division of Pearson Australia Group Pty. Ltd.)
Penguin Books India Pvt. Ltd., 11 Community Centre, Panchsheel Park, New Delhi—110 017, India
Penguin Group (NZ), 67 Apollo Drive, Rosedale, North Shore 0632, New Zealand
(a division of Pearson New Zealand Ltd.)
Penguin Books (South Africa) (Pty.) Ltd., 24 Sturdee Avenue, Rosebank, Johannesburg 2196,
South Africa

Penguin Books Ltd., Registered Offices: 80 Strand, London WC2R 0RL, England

While the author has made every effort to provide accurate telephone numbers and Internet addresses at
the time of publication, neither the publisher nor the author assumes any responsibility for errors, or for
changes that occur after publication. Further, the publisher does not have any control over and does not
assume any responsibility for author or third-party websites or their content.

PRINTING HISTORY
Perigee hardcover edition / September 2006
Perigee trade paperback edition / February 2009

Perigee trade paperback ISBN: 978-0-399-53361-7

The Library of Congress has cataloged the Perigree hardcover edition as follows:

Horn, Sam.
POP! : stand out in any crowd / by Sam Horn.— 1st ed.
p. cm.
ISBN 0-399-53276-5
1. Communication in marketing. 2. Advertising. I. Title.
HF5415.123.H68 2006
658.8'02—dc22   2006018178

PRINTED IN THE UNITED STATES OF AMERICA

10 9 8 7 6 5 4 3 2 1

Most Perigee Books are available at special quantity discounts for bulk purchases for sales promotions,
premiums, fund-raising or educational use. Special books, or book excerpts, can also be created to fit
specific needs. For details, write: Special Markets, Penguin Group (USA) Inc., 375 Hudson Street, New
York, New York 10014.

Contents

ONE: What Is POP!?

TWO: Be PURPOSEFUL

THREE: Be ORIGINAL

FOUR: Be PITHY

FIVE: Continue to POP!: Seven Secrets to Keeping Their Interest Once You've Got It

Acknowledgments

To do work you love and feel that it matters;
how could anything be more fun?
<small>KATHERINE GRAHAM</small>

My sentiments exactly. Heartfelt thanks to the following people for making it possible for me to do rewarding work I love with people I enjoy and respect.

Cheri Grimm, who runs my business so efficiently and who gives daily doses of wisdom, support, and much-needed perspective. You are an ongoing blessing in my life.

Tom and Andrew Horn, my sons who are constant sources of delight, pride, and new material and who have given me the adventure of motherhood.

Marian Lizzi and Laurie Liss, my editor and agent extraordinaire, who both believed in this book from the beginning. Thanks for being POP! cheerleaders and ambassadors.

John and Shannon Tullius, founders of the Maui Writers Conference, for kick-starting my writing career, and for our years of friendship and annual Labor Day Weekend fun.

Judy Gray, Jill Anderson, Mariah Burton Nelson, Marilynn Mobley, Rebecca Morgan, Kay Cannon, Neighbur Bert, walking buddies, insightful editors, and trusted colleagues who make every day something to look forward to.

And to all the POP! Star consulting clients and program participants for sharing your success stories. Thanks for the joyful opportunity to work with you to get your projects out of your head and into the world where they're making a positive difference for others and a prosperous living for you.

Introduction

*It's not enough to be the best at what you do; you must
be perceived as the only one who does what you do.*
JERRY GARCIA

On the first "elimination" round of FOX's 2006 *American Idol* program, a talented singer named Patrick was surprisingly voted off.

Why? As caustic judge Simon Cowell explained, "You have a good voice and you're a nice guy. You just didn't do the one thing necessary to go through to the next round. You didn't stand out from the crowd."

Yet more evidence that while talent is important, it's not enough.

Have you ever thrown your heart, mind, soul, and cash into a dream project, only to discover the world did not beat a path to your door?

Join the club. Contrary to the promise of *Field of Dreams*, if you build it, people won't necessarily come . . . *unless* you can quickly establish why you're worthwhile. If what we're offering doesn't make an immediate positive impression, people will "vote" with their feet and move on to the next thing.

You may be thinking, "You're preaching to the choir. I know it's important to stand out; I just don't know how to do it."

You're in luck. This book teaches you how.

HOW DID POP! ORIGINATE?

Find something only you can say.
JAMES DICKEY

The importance of being able to capture people's attention in sixty seconds or less became crystal clear to me the first year I emceed the Maui Writers Conference. We were proud to give budding authors from around the world a chance to meet face-to-face with publishing decision makers. This was an unprecedented opportunity for writers to pitch their books to respected agents and editors who had the power to give their projects a green light.

I'll always remember one woman who emerged from her meeting with tears in her eyes. I asked, "What happened?"

"I walked in and gave the editor my manuscript," she said. "He took one look at it and told me, 'I don't have time to read all that. Just tell me in a couple sentences what your book is about and why people will want to read it.'"

"My mind went blank," she said. "I thought it was *his* job to figure out how to sell it. I just tried to write the best novel I could."

During the rest of that conference, I discovered she wasn't the only one who thought the quality of her work would speak for itself. Other authors also seemed to believe that if they had succeeded in producing a quality project, it would elicit interest. Wrong.

There are hundreds of thousands of well-written books. The point was, how was hers different? Why would it break out from all the other books on the shelves? What was a succinct sales sound bite that would motivate busy people to try it and buy it?

My heart went out to those discouraged individuals whose dreams had been shattered, not because their work wasn't worthy, but because they hadn't known they needed to (or hadn't known how to) succinctly prove *why* it was worthy.

I started helping authors prepare sixty-second "Tell 'n Sell" pitches that articulated the commercial viability of their projects in a way decision makers "got" it and "wanted" it. News spread about my clients' success, and other individuals and organizations started hiring me to strategize how they and their projects could break out instead of blend in.

I developed my own intellectual capital called POP!, outlining how to make yourself, your cause, campaign, business, brand, product, or proposal POP! out of the pack. Since then, I've had an opportunity to work with hundreds of entrepreneurs, professionals, and creative artists to help them develop innovative titles, taglines, elevator introductions, and approaches that have helped them and their offerings become one of a kind instead of one of many.

WHAT ARE THE BENEFITS OF POP?

Let's give 'em something to talk about.
FROM BONNIE RAITT'S SONG
"SOMETHING TO TALK ABOUT"

Whether you are introducing yourself at a networking function, talking to prospective clients at a trade show, pitching your novel or screenplay, writing articles or web copy, creating an ad or commercial, naming a business or product, producing a sound-bite slogan for your cause or campaign, interviewing for a job, or competing for a contract at a bid meeting, *your success depends on whether you quickly capture your target audience's interest.* Are they sufficiently intrigued in the first sixty seconds to want to know more? Did you succeed in getting your project's foot in their mental door?

People today are so busy, so bombarded with information, that's all the time we have. If we don't convince them in our one-minute window of opportunity that we're worth their valuable time, money, and attention, they'll switch their focus to something else.

The premise of POP! is that the best way to attract instant interest is to make our communication (in particular our titles, taglines, elevator introductions, and sales slogans) Purposeful, Original, and Pithy. This is so rarely done, it makes what we're saying and selling incredibly appealing.

My goal was to remove the mystery from this "art and science of intrigue." I wanted to develop a step-by-step system *anyone* could use to win buy-in for themselves, their ideas, inventions, projects and products, causes and campaigns, businesses, and brands.

POP! is accomplishing its mission. You're about to read fun and fascinating success stories from a wide variety of people who have used these techniques to come up with innovative approaches and pitches that helped them and their offerings get noticed, heard, and bought. As four-time Pulitzer Prize nominee Fawn Germer says, "You don't have to be a creative genius to use Sam's techniques; however, using her techniques can make you a creative genius."

WHAT'S THE BEST WAY TO USE THIS BOOK?

The object of education isn't knowledge; it's action.
THOMAS KEMPIS

My hope is that you'll find this book full of practical ideas that can fast-forward the success of your ideas and inventions, and help you establish POP! of Mind Awareness with your target audiences.

Please identify something in particular you'd like to brainstorm as you read this book. What do you want people to try and buy?

What is a project or product you want noticed? An idea you want approved? A proposal you want funded?

Texas Congresswoman Barbara Jordan said, "Anyone who waits for recognition is criminally naive." If you have a concept, cause, or company you care about, it is up to you to package it in a way that captures people's attention and respect. Its quality won't speak for itself. It's your responsibility to make sure it gets the positive recognition it deserves. The good news is the techniques in this book teach you how to transform your offerings into something so appealing people want to know more.

Each chapter (1) introduces a specific POP! technique, (2) shares real-life examples showing how that technique works in a variety of situations, and (3) ends with a step-by-step, how-to exercise showing how you can apply that technique to produce your own sales sound bites and compelling communication.

If you try a technique and nothing crystallizes, simply move on to the next chapter. Sometimes the perfect title and tagline appear quickly; other times you may need to combine several techniques before you have a breakthrough.

Author Anne Sexton said, "It might take me ten pages of nothing, of terrible writing, and then I'll get a line and think, 'That's what I mean!'" And as one of my clients told me, "As long as I keep noodling, my mind continues to synthesize options and I'll eventually come up with something that didn't exist moments before. If I give in to 'premature evaluation,' my mind shuts down and I might as well hang it up."

Ready to learn how to get your ideas, products, and services noticed . . . for all the right reasons? Turn the page and let's get started.

ONE

What Is POP!?

*Keep in mind that you're more interested in
what you have to say than anyone else is.*

ANDY ROONEY

The Goal Is to Break Out, Not Blend In

There are few times in your life when it isn't too melodramatic to say your destiny hangs on the impression you make.

BARBARA WALTERS

A British journalist named Lynne Truss grew weary of the misspellings and poor punctuation she observed in grocery stores and on movie marquees. She wrote a book about the importance of using proper grammar, but anticipated it would be a tough sell because she knew most people didn't share her passion for this topic.

This was a classic POP! challenge. She had created something she believed had value, but now had to capture the attention of people who weren't particularly interested in what she had to say. Truss managed to turn her book into a bestseller by giving it a title that made it a word of mouth phenomenon.

The title that launched a thousands lips is based on the punch line to this joke: "A panda walks into a bar, orders and eats a meal, pulls out a six-shooter, fires it into the air, and starts to walk out. The puzzled waiter looks at him and asks, 'Why?' The panda throws a poorly punctuated dictionary on the table and says, 'I'm a panda.

Look it up.' The waiter finds the definition and reads, 'Panda: Large black and white mammal, indigenous to China. Food source: eats, shoots, and leaves.'"

Truss's title, *Eats, Shoots & Leaves*, catapulted her book into the international spotlight. Imagine what would have happened if she had called it *The Importance of Proper Punctuation*. That's the power of giving your idea or invention a POP! title. It takes a product that might have sold to relatives and turns it into a global phenomenon.

POP! has three components. Let's explore each of these in a little more detail.

P STANDS FOR PURPOSEFUL

*Dullness won't sell your product, but
neither will irrelevant brilliance.*
BILL BERNBACH

Communication that features brilliant wordplay doesn't qualify for POP! status unless it does two things: accurately articulates the essence of you and your offering, and positions you positively with your target audience.

Every year a few dozen courageous companies pay big bucks (an average of $2.5 million per thirty-second slot in 2006) to advertise at the Super Bowl, the international sweepstakes of high-profile commercials. The question is, how many viewers are actually motivated to try or buy the products featured in those ads? How many even remember the name of the product in the commercial that caused their uproarious laughter?

Most of us don't have millions to spend. We have to make sure that any advertisement we place, any introduction we give, any product we create, any cause or campaign we devote ourselves to delivers a high ROI (return on investment).

That's why the first requirement of a POP! pitch is that it's purposeful. If people are scratching their heads after we've introduced our idea or invention, wondering what this has to do with them, we've just wasted their time and ours.

One way to create a purposeful pitch is to place your product or business name in your slogan so it's imprinted on people's brains every time they hear or see it. For example, fill in the blank, "I wish I were an _____ _____ Wiener." Even if you haven't heard that jingle in years, you probably said, "Oscar Meyer." Now that's a POP! slogan that delivers a high ROI.

An insurance giant ensures consumers think of them every time they hear the phrase, "You're in good hands with _____." Did you say, "Allstate?" That is a perfect example of how an effective POP! slogan can accomplish its purpose every time it's said or read.

O STANDS FOR ORIGINAL

You've got to be a good date for the reader.
KURT VONNEGUT

The premise of POP! is that you've got to be a good date for your customers. It's almost a given that no matter what you're saying or selling, you're one of many. You're one of many delis, dentists, department stores, or dog walkers. One of many booths at a trade show. One of many applicants applying for a job. One of many organizations competing for your customers' business. What is it about you that distinguishes you from your competition?

One way to distinguish yourself (and be a good date for decision makers) is to be original and offer something unlike anyone or anything else. Instead of competing in a crowded niche, create your own. When you're one of a kind, there is no competition.

If you want to take dance classes and you scan the Yellow Pages, you'll see dozens of options that look much the same. But there's only one studio called *Floor Play*, and that original name may be just enough incentive for you to try them first.

People are yearning for something fresh. They welcome novelty and are delighted when we pleasantly surprise them with an uncommon approach. You may think that's hard to do because there's nothing new under the sun.

Sure there is.

Originality is alive and well. Spencer Koppel, a self-confessed nerd, realized that techies and pocket-protector types are a breed of their own. He decided to develop a website and online social network so they could meet kindred souls who share their interests. Their online personal ads don't feature romantic descriptions of drinking piña coladas while strolling along the beach, and they don't feature photos because Koppel says, "Geeks don't care about that." They do feature tongue-in-cheek profiles such as "Tall, Dork, and Handsome." What did Koppel call his site? *Geek 2 Geek* (www.gk2gk.com).

Did that name bring a smile to your face? When we see or hear something original, we find it appealing. That product or business is no longer inanimate or boring. Instead of dismissing it, we're compelled to try it. If we have a good experience, we're motivated to tell other people about it. We become word-of-mouth ambassadors who build buzz for our object of affection. All this happened because the creator invested the thought-time and brainpower to give his invention an intriguing name that helped it POP! out.

The Society of Young Jewish Professionals in Washington, DC, wanted their annual holiday party to break out of the dozens of events scheduled during December. Instead of being content to call it something mundane, the organizing committee put their heads together and came up with a catchy name that's helped it become a huge success. How huge? *USA Today* called their dance (which is open to people of all nationalities, races, and backgrounds) "the No. 1 holiday party in the nation."

So what is the original moniker that made this a must-attend event? *Matzo Ball.*

P STANDS FOR PITHY

No sinner was ever saved . . . after the
first twenty minutes of the sermon.
MARK TWAIN

The word *pithy*, which means concise and precise, may not sound very eloquent, but it's an important part of POP! communication.

The human brain can hold only approximately seven bits of information in short-term memory. If our description of our offering is longer than seven words, chances are people won't be able to remember it. And if they don't remember what we said, our effort to obtain their attention, support, and money for our offering has failed.

The top slogans of the twentieth century, as selected by *Advertising Age* magazine, are all less than seven words, proving that, when it comes to pitching, brevity is the soul of success.

- "Diamonds are forever." (De Beers)
- "Just do it." (Nike)
- "Breakfast of champions." (Wheaties)
- "We try harder." (Avis)
- "Where's the beef?" (Wendy's)

Comedian Steven Wright said, "My grandfather invented Cliff Notes in 1912. He thought of it . . . Well, to make a long story short."

When people ask, "What do you do?" or "Why should I buy this?" it's your job to make a long story short. It is your responsibility to give a clear description of what you have to offer. In Chapter 5, you'll learn how to condense a complex explanation into a Tell 'n Sell intro that motivates people to say, "Tell me more."

I can think of no finer example of a title or tagline that is both original and purposeful than the one that thirteen-year-old Jack Mc-Shane created for his grassroots cause. Following Hurricane Katrina, New Orleans officials, in a controversial decision, were forced to abandon City Park because they didn't have the funds to clean it up. Jack, who grew up across the street, said, "It bothered me to see it in such terrible condition. I thought, 'Somebody should do something about it.' Then I realized, 'I'm somebody. I should do something about it.'"

Jack got the family lawnmower out of the garage, fired it up, and went across the street to the park. Neighbors complimented him on what he was doing, so he recruited some buddies to help out. One was named Ron, so they decided to call themselves the Mow-Rons. They even created a slogan, "The Mow-Rons are in City Park; the idiots are in City Hall."

The media got wind of Jack's efforts, and he was interviewed in newspapers and on TV. His edgy slogan got laughs, but it bothered Jack because it didn't accurately represent his mission, which was to remind people that everyone has an opportunity and an obligation to contribute to their community. He kept brainstorming until he came up with something more congruent. The new title and tagline? *Weeding by Example*. Kudos.

TEST-MARKET YOUR COMMUNICATION WITH THE EYEBROW TEST

I have a photographic memory. I just haven't developed it yet.
JONATHAN WINTERS

Want to know how to tell if you've composed a successful POP! title and tagline? Just share it with people and see if it passes the Eyebrow Test.

If you've seen the movie *Jerry Maguire* (starring Tom Cruise and Renée Zellweger), you may remember toward the end when Tom's character realizes he can't live without Renée's character. He bursts into her home, rushes over to her, and starts professing his love. She patiently waits for him to stop talking so she can respond, but he keeps carrying on. Finally, she can't stand it anymore and interrupts him with, "Stop, just stop. You had me at hello."

You can instantly evaluate the commercial viability of your title and tagline anytime you want, for free. Just give people your pitch and watch their eyebrows.

If their eyebrows go up, it means your title and tagline "has them at hello." It means they're intrigued. Their curiosity has been piqued. They may even say, "Tell me more."

If their eyebrows knit or furrow, it means you have *lost* them at hello. They're confused. And when people are confused, they rarely ask for clarification. They'll either paste a polite smile on their face or utter an indifferent "oh." What's worse, they may move on and start talking about something else, not knowing or caring that you have something to offer that could benefit them.

You can also tell if your message *loses* them at hello. They may scrunch their eyes or knit their eyebrows together, a sure sign of consternation. They may paste polite smiles on their faces or nod noncommittally. They may utter an indifferent "oh" or even look away because they don't know what to say. Worst of all, they won't ask for clarification. People who are confused usually won't admit it. They just move on, not understanding or caring that what we have to offer might be of interest or use to them.

After reading their reaction, ask them to repeat what you've said. *If they can't repeat it, they didn't get it.* And if they didn't get your message, you won't get their business. If they can't remember the name of your product, how will they find it on the web or in a store? If they can't describe what your company does, why would they seek out your services? If they can't articulate your cause, why would they contribute to it? If they don't understand the gist of your proposal, why would they approve it?

In the pages ahead, you'll learn how to create Purposeful, Original, Pithy messages that give people something to talk about . . . and re- member. As Jonathan Winters pointed out, most people don't have photographic memories. It's up to us to create sales sound bites that are appealing and memorable. Are you ready to learn how to do that? Onward.

TWO

Be PURPOSEFUL

If you don't know where you're going,
you'll end up somewhere else.

Yogi Berra

2

Address and Answer the Ws

I have six honest servants; they've taught me all I know. Their
names are what, why, and who, and when and where and how.
ROBERT LOUIS STEVENSON

My walking buddy Robin is a member of a professional networking group (BNI) that meets every week at a local restaurant. Their purpose is to support each other by exchanging best-practice tips, business leads, and lessons learned. She told me that her first meeting left quite an impression because she saw the worst and best member showcase she's ever witnessed, back to back.

The first individual got up and droned on about his services, which Robin still doesn't understand to this day. She told me she never knew ten minutes could be so long.

Then a woman named Michele Powers, owner of a business called NutrientChef, got up. Instead of blathering on about her business, she brought up four strategically selected clients who enthusiastically explained why hiring Michele had been one of the smartest investments they'd ever made.

One woman proudly revealed how much weight she'd lost now that Michele prepared delicious, portion-correct meals for her. A man who worked sixty hours a week said he'd stopped picking up fast food on the way home from work because he knew there would be something he wanted to eat waiting for him in the refrigerator. As a result, his cholesterol and blood pressure had both dropped.

A working couple told how relieved they were to serve balanced, pre-prepared meals to their family instead of coming home exhausted and having to fix something from scratch. A thrilled mother told her story about hiring Michele to teach her college-bound son to cook quick, healthy, inexpensive meals.

Robin told me, "At the end of the meeting, Michele was surrounded by enthusiastic people ready to hire her on the spot."

Michele's approach was brilliant because it was purposeful. She had researched her audience and knew they were tired of people standing up and simply explaining what their business did. Her "show, don't tell" testimonials captured and kept the group's interest while proving the benefits of her services, all in ten minutes.

Most of us don't have ten minutes to showcase our offering. We've got less than one minute to prove we're worth trying and buying. To do this, we must be 100 percent clear about the nine Ws:

W1. What am I offering?
W2. What problem does my idea or offering solve?
W3. Why is it worth trying and buying?
W4. Who is my target audience?
W5. Who am I and what are my credentials?
W6. Who are my competitors and how am I different from them?
W7. What resistance or objections will people have to this?
W8. What is the purpose of my pitch?
W9. When, where, and how do I want people to take action?

If you've ever worked as a salaried employee, you've heard of W2 Forms. The above is what I call your W9 Form, and it is the key to making your marketing message purposeful.

If you anticipate, address, and answer these W questions in your communication, people will get what you're saying, will be convinced it's relevant for them, and will be more likely to want what you're offering or recommending, or at least they'll be sufficiently intrigued and impressed to want to know more.

FILL OUT YOUR W9 FORM

Writing is not hard. Just get paper and pencil,
sit down, and write it as it occurs to you.
The writing is easy—it's the occurring that's hard.
Steven Leacock

You might have already thought through these W questions as they relate to your priority project. If so, good for you. Please write out your answers anyway because you will be using them throughout the book to make sure the titles, taglines, and introductions you develop are purposeful.

I have provided prompts to jump-start your thinking and make the "occurring" easier in case this is the first time you've asked yourself these W questions. The goal of this section is to give you multiple opportunities to clarify your purpose while generating a comprehensive language bank that explains what you want to say or sell. You will then pull out your Core Words (descriptive phrases that articulate the essence of your offering), which will become the basis of your POP! messages.

Please note: Answering these questions can take ten minutes or two hours, depending on how thorough you want to be. It may be tempting to fast-forward to the "fun stuff," however, I suggest you invest the time to formulate thoughtful answers to these questions, as it will pay off in the long run by positioning you for maximum success.

W1. WHAT AM I OFFERING? WHAT AM I PITCHING, RECOMMENDING, TRYING TO SELL?

Success is to have one's ideas exclusively
focused on one central interest.
SIGMUND FREUD

Remember when I asked you to select a priority project so you can apply the POP! techniques to your company or cause? What did you select? What will you be brainstorming? Are you:

- selecting a slogan for a membership or fund-raising drive for your association?
- looking for the perfect title for your song, screenplay, novel, gadget?
- developing a marketing campaign for a new product or project?
- interviewing for a job, contract, or promotion?

My offering (and the priority project that I'll be brainstorming during this book) is _____

_____

W2. WHAT PROBLEM DOES MY IDEA OR OFFERING SOLVE?

Before you build a better mousetrap, it helps to know
if there are any mice out there.
MORTIMER ZUCKERMAN

What is causing your customers pain, grief, or inconvenience? What keeps them up at night, staring at the ceiling with worry or apprehension?

- In what way are people hassled or aggrieved by this issue? How does your proposal or product alleviate that?
- What is a challenge people don't know how to face? How does your service help them deal with that successfully?
- What is causing your target audience discomfort? Are you the first or only one who knows how to fix this? Explain.

My product, process, project, or proposal addresses this problem

_____

in a unique way by doing this _____

_____

_____

W3. WHY IS IT WORTH TRYING AND BUYING?

When are you going to realize that if it doesn't apply to me, it doesn't matter?
CANDACE BERGEN ON *MURPHY BROWN*

Why will people benefit from your process or product? What will they stop, start, or do differently as a result of using your service or business?

- Will employees be able to handle customer complaints more efficiently?
- Will overweight children be motivated to eat healthier food?
- Will travelers not have to lug around heavy luggage?
- Will salespeople learn how to close more sales more quickly?

Three specific benefits people will receive for trying and buying my product, approving my proposal, or using my services include:

a) _____

b) _____

c) _____

W4. WHO IS MY TARGET AUDIENCE?

To seduce almost anyone, ask for and listen to his opinion.
MALCOLM FORBES

Who wants or needs what you're selling or suggesting? Who are you asking for their time, attention, opinion, and approval?

Don't think of the millions of people who may eventually buy your product, hire your services, or contribute to your campaign. Picture a specific individual or organization who needs or wants what you're offering.

- Age: How old is that individual? How long has this business been in operation? What are its age demographics?
- Size: Is the person petite, tall, slender, large? Is this a small "mom and pop" shop or a multinational corporation?
- Income: Is this individual wealthy? Is this family burdened with a mortgage and three college tuitions? Is the company profitable or on a tight budget?
- Morale: Is the person happy and content? Is the family dysfunctional? Is the corporation growing or is it downsizing and employees are worried sick?
- Education: Is the individual a high school dropout? Do both parents in the family have advanced degrees? Is the company comprised largely of white-collar workers?

- Characteristics: Is this individual in jail? Is this family actively involved in their church? Does this organization have a diverse workforce of many different nationalities?
- Group Dynamics: Do employees telecommute or work remotely? Are there round-the-clock work shifts? Do team leaders participate in quality circles?

My target audience—the specific individual or organization who needs what I've got—is _____

_____

W5. WHO AM I AND WHAT ARE MY CREDENTIALS?

All the wrong people have inferiority complexes.

ANONYMOUS

What in your background qualifies you to offer this? How have you "lived" this so people can trust your expertise and put their faith in you? What special experience or proven track record does your company bring to this project?

A dear friend, named Therese Godfrey, offered workshops on personal and professional goal-setting. The irony was, Therese had actually completed the Ironman Triathalon (yes, the grueling 2.4-mile swim, 100-mile bike ride, and 26.2-mile marathon held in Hawaii) but she was not using any of her Ironman stories in her programs.

When asked why, she said, "Well, that happened a long time ago. Plus, it seems like I'm bragging and I'm not comfortable doing that."

Perhaps you've heard the insight that "Our strength taken to an extreme becomes our weakness." This was a case where Therese's integrity and modesty were being taken to an extreme and keeping her from sharing this rare experience. The fact was she had completed this grueling athletic event. People would enjoy experiencing it vicariously through her.

Therese could claim an accomplishment few others could. People were impressed and curious. They *wanted* to hear about it. Plus, it was relevant to her topic of how to set a challenging goal and achieve it—no matter what.

Could you also have an achievement, attribute, or first-hand experience on which you haven't been capitalizing because it seemed liked it was a) boasting, b) old news, c) irrelevant? Could your project team have credentials you've been overlooking?

- What do you bring to the table no one else does? Where do you outshine others?
- What is a credential or type of expertise none of your competitors can claim?
- What proof or evidence do you have of that special skill or talent?
- What track record does your organization have with this type of account, contract, or product? What statistics or data prove your company's success in this area?
- What values and principles do you bring to the table? Skateboarder Tony Hawk is revered in the X-Game world because he won't compromise his principles. Is your integrity one of your biggest assets?

Special credentials or characteristics of me and/or my organization that are singular include _____

_____

_____

W6. WHO ARE MY COMPETITORS AND HOW AM I DIFFERENT FROM THEM?

When you can do the common things in an uncommon way,
you will command the attention of the world.
GEORGE WASHINGTON CARVER

Which individuals and organizations offer services or products similar to yours? Describe them and identify at least two ways you are the opposite of them. How are you uncommon? How do you not duplicate what's already available elsewhere?

WASH radio in the District of Columbia is an excellent example of a business that has successfully distinguished itself from its competition. Their claim to fame is that they are the "Do Not Repeat after Me" station. Obviously, they scoped out their competition and concluded everyone was playing the same top forty songs. To offer an alternative, they promise to never play the same song twice during working hours. Their slogan, "Do Not Repeat after Me," emphasizes how they are unlike their competition. Kind of like the *un*-cola, right?

- What are your competitors' strengths? In what way are they superior to you?
- What are their weaknesses or oversights? In what way are they inferior?
- What qualities do you have that they don't? What are your advantages? What can you deliver or promise that they can't? What is your competitive edge?
- What physical characteristics set you apart? How does your product look and sound?
- What are you doing—or what could you be doing—that is the opposite of what others in your field are doing?

Volkswagen is famous for turning an "albatross" characteristic into an asset. Instead of trying to compete with the larger, more luxurious car models (and coming up short, so to speak), their creative team turned their "ugliness" into a proud and distinctive hallmark. Their self-deprecating ads played off their "petite" size and turned it into an appealing characteristic. One of their most famous full-page ads featured almost 75 percent blank space with a small "Beetle" in the lower right-hand corner and this one-sentence caption: "It makes your house look bigger." Bravo.

My two top competitors are _____

_____

Two ways in which my product and I are different include

_____

_____

W7. WHAT RESISTANCE OR OBJECTIONS WILL PEOPLE HAVE TO THIS?

Don't fight forces; use them.
R. BUCKMINSTER FULLER

Why might people be apathetic about your idea or invention? Why might decision makers say this is risky or unreasonable? Why would people say "no thanks"?

- Will people think your product is too complicated or hard to assemble?
- Would customers question your credibility or not be convinced of your expertise?
- Has your idea already been done before and it failed or backfired?
- Are your services or product priced too high?

- What evidence do you have that this *will* work and is worth taking this risk? What are your objective and subjective reasons for continuing to pursue this?
- Have you satisfactorily addressed and/or neutralized anticipated objections? How?

People might resist my offering because _____
_____ ;
however, I've anticipated and neutralized those objections by
_____
_____

W8. WHAT IS THE PURPOSE OF MY PITCH?

Destiny is not a matter of chance, it is a matter of choice;
it is not a thing to be waited for, it is a thing to be achieved.
WILLIAM JENNINGS BRYAN

What are you primarily trying to achieve? At the end of your communication, do you want to persuade:

- the editorial board to approve and fund your pet project?
- couples to choose to come to your "date movie" this Friday night?
- college students to start a checking/savings account with your bank?

The purpose of my what (Program? Product? Proposal?) _____
_____
_____

is to (Persuade? Inspire? Educate? Entertain? Enlighten? Connect?)

_____

_____

who (VIP client? Employees? Prospective customers? Investors?
Current clients?)

_____

_____

to do what? (Hire you? Stop smoking? Invest in my start-up?)

_____

_____

W9. WHEN, WHERE, AND HOW DO I WANT PEOPLE TO TAKE ACTION?

All the beautiful sentiments in the world weigh
less than a single lovely action.
JAMES RUSSELL LOWELL

The clearer you are about your answers to this question, the more
likely it is to happen. If you are vague in "asking for the sell," people
won't know what they're supposed to do. They may agree with what
you're saying, but that won't necessarily translate into them calling,
buying, visiting, ordering, or supporting your recommendation unless they're given clear directions on how to do so. Only when you
specify the action you want people to take in measurable terms, will
you be able to evaluate the success of your pitch.

- Is there a deadline associated with your offer? Do people feel a
  sense of urgency? Is sooner better than later? Is this situation
  costing them money; putting them at risk; endangering their
  health? What are two reasons individuals or organizations

can't afford to ignore this problem, delay approval on this proposal, or procrastinate on this offer? When exactly should they follow up? Now? Next week?

- Where will people be able to buy your product, sign up for your services, order your merchandise, register for your event, vote for your candidate, contribute to your cause?
- Brick and mortar stores? Which ones? Company headquarters? Where is that?
- Websites? Which ones?
- Catalogs? Which ones? Magazines? Newspapers?
- Learning centers? Colleges? Adult education programs? Conferences?
- TV or radio? Newspapers or magazines? Which ones?
- Team of salespeople? Affiliates? Multilevel marketing? Resellers?
- How exactly are people supposed to take action? Do they write a check right now? Use a credit card online? Send in an order form? Fill out an application and submit it in person to your head office? Click on a link that takes them to the relevant page on your website? Show up at next month's meeting at a specific time and location?

I want people to take this specific action _____

_____

on or by this date _____ at this location,

website, place _____

_____

THE GOAL IS TO LEAD THE PACK, NOT FOLLOW IT

*Creativity often consists of merely turning up
what is already there.*
BERNICE FITZGIBBON

Good for you. You've clarified your Ws and come up with lots of descriptive data that comprehensively explains what it is you have to say or sell. Now it's time to review what you've produced to pinpoint how you are original. An old adage states "Imitation is the sincerest form of flattery." When it comes to marketing messages, imitation is the shortest path to failure.

You can turn a "yawner" into something eye-opening by doing the opposite, not the obvious. For forty years, customers have pounded ketchup bottles against their palm in a futile effort to pour out that slow-moving condiment. Heinz had a "duh moment" and turned its product (and industry) on its head by redesigning ketchup bottles to rest on their cap so gravity could work its magic.

Study your W9 answers and identify one specific characteristic or benefit that is *un*available elsewhere. Where are you an "un?" Focusing on that point of distinction when crafting your communication can help you quickly stand out from competitors.

The makers of the acid-reflux medication Nexium obviously understood this concept. They faced a challenge entering the highly competitive prescription drug market because there were already several established acid-reflux medications available. The ingredients were much the same, so how could they stand out? Well, there were already blue pills, white pills, yellow pills, and pink pills, but no purple pills. Rather than focusing on their not-so-easy-to-remember name, their ads focus on their "only-one-in-the-marketplace" color, suggesting you ask your doctor about the "Purple Pill."

STAY ON MESSAGE BY REFERRING TO YOUR W9 FORM

*It's hard to stay on purpose if we don't
know what our purpose is.*

SAM HORN

You have now collected language data that points out why your project is valuable and viable. Your next task is to condense your W9 Form into the POP! communication equivalent of a one-page business plan.

Your answers on the previous pages are too bulky to work with when composing your POP! marketing messages. By compressing the essential Ws into one page, you can easily refer to it when brainstorming the techniques in the upcoming chapters. When you come up with catchy titles and taglines, check them against your W9 answers to make sure they're "on purpose." Remember, clever isn't enough. Your communication must appeal to your target audience in a meaningful way that causes them to take the desired action.

Take your W9 Form with you everywhere you go. Saul Bellow said, "I never had to change a word of what I got up in the middle of the night to write." Whenever you think of a potential name or overhear a phrase that perfectly describes your process, note it under the appropriate heading. When you record each "Aha" the moment it occurs, the world becomes your material.

My Project's W9 Form

W1. What am I offering? What am I pitching, recommending, trying to sell?

_____

_____

W2. What problem does my idea or offering solve?

_____

_____

W3. Why is this worth buying or trying?

_____

_____

W4. Who is my target audience?

_____

_____

W5. Who am I and what are my credentials?

_____

_____

W6. Who are my competitors and how am I different from them?

_____

_____

W7. What resistance or objections will people have to this?

_____

_____

W8. What is the purpose of my pitch?

_____

_____

W9. When, where, and how do I want people to take action?

_____

_____

WHAT Core Words do I use to describe my business or brand?

- _____   - _____
- _____   - _____
- _____   - _____
- _____   - _____

THREE

Be ORIGINAL

You've got to be original. If you're like everybody else, what do they need you for?

BERNADETTE PETERS

3

Alphabetize Your Core Words

Life comes before literature, as the material always comes before the work. The hills are full of marble before the world blooms with statues.

PHILLIP BROOKS

The first time I gave a presentation on conflict resolution, I called it "Dealing with Difficult People—Without Becoming One Yourself."

Now, that's an okay title, but if you Google the phrase "difficult people," you find pages of resources. That would mean I'd be competing with hundreds, if not thousands, of other psychologists, consultants, and authors speaking and writing on that topic.

Luckily, there was a gentleman in the front row who didn't get up at the first break to get some fresh air or a cup of coffee. He just sat there, gazing off into space. I was curious and went over to ask what he was thinking.

He said, "I'm a real estate broker. I took this workshop because I deal with some very demanding people. They seem to think they can treat me any way they want, and I'm tired of it. I thought I would learn some zingers to fire back at them and put them in their place. That's not what this is about, is it?" He continued, "I'm a student of martial arts. I've studied karate, tae kwan do, judo. What you're suggesting is like a verbal form of kung fu, isn't it?"

"You're right," I said, "it's kind of like a . . . Tongue Fu!" Eureka. The perfect name.

When you coin your own term for a topic, you haven't just come up with a clever title, you are now positioned to create a business empire. You can trademark that title, license people to teach your methodology, create proprietary products that produce passive income, and build a business you can sell because it has equity.

Once you create an original word, don't stop there. Run the word through the alphabet, changing the sound of the first syllable to match the corresponding letter. For example, if you Alphabetize *Tongue Fu!*, you get:

Fun Fu!—how to handle hassles with humor instead of harsh words

Run Fu!—alternative strategies for when Tongue Fu! doesn't work

Tongue Sue!—Tongue Fu! tips for lawyers

Young Fu!—Tongue Fu! techniques for dealing with kids

Each of those titles could be a chapter in a book, an e-book, or developed into a teleseminar, CD series, or presentation tailored to its specific target audience.

COIN A ONE-OF-A-KIND NAME

Never change a winning game, always change a losing one.
VINCE LOMBARDI

Is your company or product's current name winning new customers? If so, good for you. If it isn't, why not change it to something better? One way to come up with a name that wins buy-in is to run your Core Words through the alphabet, changing the sound of the first syllable to match the corresponding letter. The result (think "mock-umentary" for a satirical documentary, or "hacktivists" for computer enthusiasts who are battling Internet censorship) can produce a new word that belongs to you and you alone, and that helps your idea or invention become the "next new thing."

For example, General Mills and Yoplait wanted a name for their new product that packaged yogurt in no-muss, no-fuss squeeze tubes. All they had to do was run their Core Word "yogurt" through the alphabet . . .

Ao-gurt (Nope.)
Bo-gurt
Co-gurt (Keep going.)
Do-gurt
Eo-gurt (Not yet.)
Fo-gurt
Go-gurt

Go-gurt! A perfect name that reinforces their marketing message that this health food turned fast food is an ideal option for people who want to eat right when on the run.

If you've invented a revolutionary product, it deserves to have a revolutionary name. If you want your product to POP! off the shelf, it's got to have a name that POP!s off the packaging. For example, I saw some lined notepads with the words "Do Not Forget" at the top. Big whoop. How much would you pay for that? Maybe a dollar or two?

But that rather ordinary product was cleverly designed to be hung on a doorknob, much like the "Do Not Disturb" signs placed on hotel doorknobs. This creative shape and specialized purpose transformed a common pad of paper into an interesting and useful gift for memory-challenged people. The creators made it even more appealing, proprietary, and profitable by giving it a POP! name— *Forget Me Not(e)s.*

Humorist Dave Barry writes an annual column in December describing unusual gifts readers have brought to his attention. One of my favorites described a father whose toddlers constantly begged him to get down on all fours so they could climb on his back and pretend to play "horsie." Unfortunately, they kept falling off as he galloped around the room. This innovative father had a brainstorm and decided to design a special parent-sized saddle to cinch on his back so his kids could climb on board and ride to their heart's content.

I bet you can figure out what he called his contraption. Simply take his Core Word "saddle" and run it through the alphabet, changing the pronunciation of the first syllable to match the corresponding letter. Let's see, there's Addle, Baddle, Caddle, *Daddle*! Yup. That's what he called it. In less than one minute and with *zero* marketing budget, he conjured up a POP! name that catapulted his creation into the limelight.

Another item in Dave's column featured a clever gift for lovers who didn't want to take their gloves off in winter to hold hands. This inventor designed a conjoined mitten so they could walk hand-in-hand without freezing their fingers off. Simply run "mitten" through the alphabet and see what you come up with. Aitten, bitten, citten, ditten, eitten, fittin . . . Keep going and you arrive at . . . *Smitten*! That novel name brings a smile to your face and a reach for your wallet.

ARE YOU PUSHING YOUR CREATIVE ENVELOPE?

Have I really pushed the envelope as much as I want to?
Not yet. That's why I'm still creatively hungry.
STEVEN SPIELBERG

Instead of pushing the creative envelope, why not create a new one? About ten years ago, the scuba industry in Hawaii was tanking (sorry, couldn't resist). The problem was that you needed a current scuba certification, which meant a lot of people who wanted to explore the beautiful underwater reefs couldn't.

An enterprising shop owner had a revelation. Why not run long air hoses from the dive boat that divers could keep in their mouths, kind of like elongated snorkels? That way, they could "breathe easy" and swim with the fishes to their heart's content. There's no risk because they'd only be ten to fifteen feet below and they could resurface in seconds if necessary. Plus, divers wouldn't have to haul around a heavy oxygen tank or go through the costly, time-consuming certification. *Anyone* could do this.

This innovative idea spawned a multimillion-dollar industry—partially because this visionary used his imagination to solve a problem people were having (Question #2 on the W9 Form) and partially because he gave this brand-new activity a brand-new name that's fun-to-say and easy-to-remember. Will you forget *Snuba*?

Art gallery owners in New York have found it pays to hire beautiful young women to attend their openings because it draws a crowd who want to see and be seen with the "beautiful people." What do they call these models and ballet dancers who do this to earn extra money? Gallerinas.

GENERATE FREE MEDIA ATTENTION WITH CLEVER NAMES

A man should learn to watch that gleam of light which flashes across his mind from within.
RALPH WALDO EMERSON

Are you thinking, "Big deal, so these are clever names"? You bet it's a big deal. The media is always looking for the next new thing. You don't need a hefty advertising budget. You can be featured in publications around the country if you come up with an attention-grabbing name.

A restaurant-bar in Alexandria, Virginia, wanted to attract more customers. With hundreds of restaurants in the Washington, DC, area, they needed something out of the ordinary to give people a reason to choose them. They found it by noticing one of their customers kept tying his loyal Lab to the lamppost outside before coming in for a beer.

Why not have a happy hour for local professionals who were out walking their dogs after returning home from a long day at work? This enterprising Holiday Inn fixed up their outdoor patio and put out water bowls and dog biscuits for the canine set. They deserve kudos for their innovative idea, but I'm convinced it was the clever Alphabetized name that turned this into a popular tradition and media favorite. Run *happy hour* through the alphabet and what do you (eventually) come up with? *Yappy Hour.*

Yappy Hour caught the attention of the *Washington Post*, which wrote a flattering article about this "petworking" (dog owners networking) opportunity. The event became even more popular and profitable. Dozens of newspapers around the country ran that article and now millions of people know about the Holiday Inn's Yappy Hour in Alexandria, Virginia—all because the manager invested a little brainpower and wasn't content to blend in.

TRY SPELL CHUCK

*I don't give a damn for a man who can
only spell a word one way.*
Mark Twain

You've heard of spell check? I suggest you try Spell Chuck. Discard the "normal" way of spelling to create terms that are brand new—and that belong only to you.

For example, there are thousands of volunteer groups across the country. When Disney was looking for a name for its community-oriented service program, they wanted a unique name that reinforced their brand icon of Mickey Mouse. The result? *VoluntEARS*.

For whatever reason (probably because there are so many shops in any given area and they're desperate to differentiate themselves), beauty salons seem to be good practitioners of Spell Chuck. There's *Shear Genius. Curl up and Dye. Cut and Dried.*

Another variation of the Alphabetizing technique is to substitute a relevant phrase that sounds sufficiently similar to the first syllable of one of your Core Words.

For example, *entrepreneur* can be transformed into a variety of trademarkable terms. There's *Zenpreneur*, a spiritual small business owner. I've coined a term for writers who take responsibility for promoting their books: *Authorpreneurs*, and for people who make their living from their mind: *Ideapreneurs*. A celebrity chef could call himself an *Entréepreneur*.

ARE YOU THE MASTER OF YOUR DOMAIN?

Find what gave you emotion, what action gave you excitement.
Then write it down, making it clear so the reader can see it too.
ERNEST HEMINGWAY

When you form a new word, don't just get excited and write it down. Go immediately to your computer and bring up www.go daddy.com or its equivalent. GoDaddy is my favorite resource for registering sites because for $8.95 (as of 2008 when I'm writing this book) you can reserve a domain name (if it's available). You then "own" that URL for the period of time you've paid for, which can range from one to ten years.

Please note: This isn't a trademark and you still need to develop that website with strategically developed content that ranks you highly search engines. This just protects the name and means no one else can set up a website with "your" URL and proprietary phrase.

Protecting your intellectual property is becoming increasingly important as we become more dependent on electronic commerce. If you have a product and don't have its related domain name, you don't really own your financial future. If someone hears about your business, chances are they'll head to the web to check you out. You want to be sure they bring up your site, not a competitor's. If people see you on TV or hear you on the radio, they may not remember your name, but if they remember even a key word of what you said (e.g., teenage mothers, flu vaccine, day-trading), they can enter that word into their favorite search engine and your website will come up.

Interestingly, GoDaddy.com is itself a POP! name. Initially called Jomax Technologies, owner Bob Parsons changed it to Go-Daddy because, "It was more memorable, kind of fun, and had a retro sort of sound to it." Good call, Bob. The business is on its way to becoming a billion-dollar company, thanks in part to its fun and easy-to-say name, which gives the impression it will be fun and easy to use.

WANT TO GET NOTICED?
COIN NEW WORDS

All words are pegs to hang ideas on.
HENRY WARD BEECHER

The Alphabetizing technique can also be used to spice up interviews and give the press interesting sound bites to feature in their promo spots. I was watching the X Games on TV with my teenage sons. In a special feature, Motocross champion Jeremy McGrath took a camera crew to his "crib" to show them his 3,500-square-foot garage with its impressive variety of expensive cars, gleaming motorcycles, and tricked-out snowmobiles. The reporter was amazed by how luxurious it was and burst out with, "Wow, it's kind of like the Taj Mahal." Without missing a beat, Jeremy quipped, "Yeah, we call it the *Garage Mahal*!"

You may be thinking, "Okay, that was clever. So what?" That network probably shot dozens of hours of interviews with those X Games stars. Of all the footage shot, who got featured? McGrath's grateful sponsors were no doubt pleased with that added exposure to millions of extreme-sports fans.

Remember this when being interviewed by the media, introducing yourself at an industry event, or representing your company at a trade show. The pithier and more interesting your sound bite, the more likely it will be featured, remembered, and repeated.

HOW TO USE THE ALPHABETIZING TECHNIQUE

Creativity may simply be the realization that there's no particular virtue to doing things the way they've always been done.
RUDOLF FLESCH

Ready to do this for yourself? Just follow these steps and let your imagination do the rest.

Step 1. Get out your project's W9 Form and your list of Core Words.

Step 2. Take one Core Word at a time and "talk it" through the alphabet, changing the sound of the first syllable to match the corresponding letter—starting with A and working to Z. Do this out loud so you can sound out the "new" words to hear if they POP!

Step 3. Write down any phrases that sound as if they could be turned into something meaningful. List them even if you're not sure if or how you can use them. You can play with them later and use different techniques to morph them into something proprietary.

Step 4. Keep experimenting with the new combinations that "appear" before your eyes. For example, what do you call it when a teenager has a haughty attitude? *Bratitude.* When I was in Alaska, I saw an ad for a business that flies tourists in small float planes to remote lakes and mountain valleys in Alaska. Simply ask yourself, What does this business do? They take visitors sightseeing. Now, run *sightseeing* through the alphabet and you come up with *fightseeing.* Make a creative leap with Spell Chuck and there it is . . . *Flightseeing.* Try this technique to generate clever slogans for local businesses you see advertised in the newspaper. It's great practice and a lot of fun.

From now on, don't bury your offering by giving it a generic name or ho-hum description that makes it look and sound like everything else. Give yourself a competitive edge by Alphabetizing your Core Words to create a one-of-a-kind name that helps it POP! off the page, shelf, or screen in that crucial one-minute window of opportunity.

4

Capture Conversational
Catchphrases

*A good conversationalist is not one who remembers what was
said, but someone who says what people want to remember.*
JOHN MASON BROWN

Career coach Julie Jansen wanted to write a book about finding
your ideal work, but felt many of the good titles were already
taken. "There's *What Color is Your Parachute?*, *Take This Job and Love
It*, *Do What You Love and the Money Will Follow*. Everything I come up
with is boring compared to those."

I simply asked her, "What do clients tell you when they come
into your office? What do you frequently hear from participants in
your programs?" She thought about it for a moment and then her
face lit up. "You know what I hear a lot? 'I don't know what I want,
but I know it's not this.'"

"That's your title," I said. "Imagine you're in a bookstore in the
career section and you're looking for just the right book to help you
figure out what you want to do with the rest of your life. You're doing the bookstore shuffle (you know what I mean, you have your
head tilted to one side so you can read the titles of the books on the
spines and you're shuffling your feet as you work your way down the

row). *Build a Rewarding Career. Job Search Techniques*. Suddenly, you see *I Don't Know What I Want, But I Know It's Not This*. Wouldn't you be compelled to take the book off the shelf and look through it? Wouldn't you think, 'Now *this* author knows how I feel. This is the book for me.' That's the power of a Conversational Catchphrase title."

If you want a playful way to create communication people instantly relate to and remember, simply ask yourself, What is a common challenge facing people who need my service? What are they frustrated with? Put yourself in the minds of people in the middle of that situation. Now, start talking out loud. Write every thought that comes to mind. Review what you've written, pick out a phrase that articulates your customers' exasperation or heartfelt emotion, and feature it in your pitch or proposal.

The creative team at www.zappos.com, a popular online shoe store, did just this to pinpoint a common complaint about their industry. They put themselves "in the shoes" of target buyers and found many were tired of trying to track down a department store employee willing to go "in back" and hunt down shoes customers could try on in their size. With that in mind, Zappos recently ran a full-page ad that featured a huge headline that trumpeted, "You know those salespeople who treat you like you don't exist? They don't work here." Now there's a company in step with its customers' needs.

Put yourself in the figurative shoes of your customers. What are they saying to themselves when they're contemplating using your service? Imagine you are a chiropractor. What is the first thing patients complain about or say when they walk into your clinic? "Oh, my aching back?!!" That might be a more resonant headline for an ad, article, or banner for your website homepage than "Why You Should See a Chiropractor."

ARE YOU LISTENING TO YOUR CUSTOMERS?

My girlfriend says I never listen to her. I think that's what she said.
DRAKE SATHER

Are you featuring your client's repeated feedback in the description of what you have to offer? If so, great. If not, why not? They are giving you your name, slogan, or pitch. It is what they associate with you. Why use something different when your target audience is already telling you what works for them?

Another career coach initially resisted this idea because she didn't like the catchphrase she kept hearing. Robin Palangin needed a motto for her business, My Authentic Career. A frustration she heard frequently from people was "I wish I knew what I wanted to be when I grow up!"

I asked why she wasn't using that line in her marketing message and she said, "My clients *are* grown up. I think it would offend them to infer they're not."

I countered, "Think about it, Robin. This is what they're saying, which means it's an area of concern. If you highlight that phrase on your website, people will want to work with you because they'll believe you can help them figure out what to do about this."

Robin decided to experiment with that line on her homepage and was immediately rewarded with a dramatic increase in inquiries. She was amazed at how many people said, "Sign me up for that retreat. I knew as soon as I saw that line that this was for me."

In addition to listening to what people say when facing current challenges, you can also anticipate what they would *like* to be able to say when this challenge is finally resolved.

A classic Crest ad featured a "What would our customers *like* to say?" sound bite. What would parents most love to hear when their kids walked out of the dentist's office? "Look, Ma. No cavities!" Now that's a slogan that strikes a chord with consumers.

SEE YOUR SITUATION THROUGH YOUR CUSTOMERS' EYES

My wife made me get these glasses. I wasn't seeing things her way.
MARK KLEIN

Darian Rashid, managing director of VR Data Systems in New Jersey, told me about a time early in his career when he and his college roommate were seeking venture capital to fund an innovative software system they had designed. They had hired a well-known marketing consultant to help them pitch their product to a wealthy financial firm famous for bankrolling start-ups.

Although Darian and his partner were brilliant techies, they were in their twenties. Their marketing consultant was concerned about their relative youth and told them to sit in the back of the room and keep quiet while he presented the pitch. What's worse, he ordered them *not* to demonstrate the software because these "money guys wouldn't be able to understand it." The consultant then launched into his fancy PowerPoint presentation, complete with complicated graphs and confusing statistics.

Darian found himself sinking in his chair as he watched the bankers get more and more confused. He saw the deal disappearing right in front of him and decided he had nothing to lose. He jumped out of his chair and said, "Here, let me show you how it works." Despite a daggered look from the consultant, Darian sat at the computer and, fingers flying over the keys, started showing, with pride and passion, how his "baby" worked.

An older gentleman, who had been sitting in the hall outside the meeting room, walked in and started watching Darian's demonstration with great interest. After a few minutes, he burst out, "That's so simple, my mother could do it!"

As luck would have it, this older gentleman happened to be the president of the bank and the decision maker on the deal. Not only did Darian get his funding, the exclamation "So simple, your mother can use it" became their marketing message.

Did you see the movie *When Harry Met Sally?* (I know, I'm dating myself here.) A classic scene in that movie features Meg Ryan's character Sally confessing to Billy Crystal's character Harry over lunch that many women fake orgasms. At first, Harry doesn't believe her and claims that no one has ever done so with him because he "would know."

Smiling, Sally challenges him and claims he wouldn't be able to tell the difference. She then launches into a demonstration right there in the deli, complete with moans and little yelps of ecstasy. The scene is funny, but what caps it off is when a woman at the next table (actually director Rob Reiner's mother) watches this unfold and then says dryly to her waiter, "I'll have what she's having."

Ask yourself, What do people say when they're exultant or triumphant about something dealing with my product? Write down these "Eureka!" exclamations because other people will want that for themselves.

A participant in one of my POP! presentations wanted to write, speak, and consult about male-female communication, but knew that bestselling authors John Gray (*Men Are from Mars, Women Are from Venus*) and Deborah Tannen (*You Just Don't Understand*) already have POP! of Mind Awareness with media and meeting planners on that topic, so she needed to come up with an imaginative title if she wanted to get noticed and get booked.

I suggested we use the Conversational Catchphrase technique and asked the attendees in the room to pretend they were trying to communicate with a member of the opposite sex. I told them, "You're a man or you're a woman. You're trying to get your point across, but you're getting aggravated because they don't seem to be listening. Start saying out loud what you're thinking."

The room was instantly abuzz with catchphrases that articulated their impatience and irritation, an ideal source of heartfelt messages. Finally, a guy in the back of the room shouted out the winning title, "Can't she see I'm watching the game?"

If you're writing a song about love, simply ask yourself, What do singles say when it's late at night and they're tempted to go home with someone they're attracted to? (By the way, that sample scenario produced a memorable lyric, "I may hate myself in the morning, but I'm going to love you tonight," in a popular country-western tune.)

ARE YOU CAPTURING YOUR CUSTOMERS' EXCLAMATIONS?

You Are SO Not Invited to My Bat Mitzvah!
TITLE OF A BOOK BY FIONA ROSENBLOOM

Have you noticed a trend? Titles and slogans that elicit a visceral reaction are often the ones in which there's an implied or actual exclamation, a phrase uttered vehemently with immediacy and emotion.

Ask yourself, What do my target customers *exclaim* when they are upset about "my" issue? What do they burst out saying when facing this predicament? What do they think to themselves, but are afraid to 'fess up to?

That could be an ideal title or slogan. You are increasing the likelihood your target audience will instantly identify with it because it's couched in the same language they use. The visceral truth of your catchphrase will cause people to almost involuntarily respond, "That's exactly how I feel!"

Be sure to ask clients to fill out comment cards and evaluations. When customers share compliments about what a difference your product or service has made for them, be sure to ask for permission to use their remarks. Endorsements such as "I'm so glad I bought your product because . . ." or "This is the best . . ." offer persuasive proof to prospective customers that you can be trusted to deliver quality results. Be sure to feature those catchphrase endorsements in your marketing material, in your introduction, and on your website. Third-party testimonials are often the first thing people read when deciding whether to buy your item, hire your services, or do business with your company.

HOW TO USE THE CONVERSATIONAL CATCHPHRASE TECHNIQUE

The debt we owe to the play of the imagination is incalculable.
CARL JUNG

Don't put undue pressure on yourself by trying to *think up* a brilliant title or slogan. That's a logical approach that kills creativity. Simply use the Conversational Catchphrase technique to *think back* to when you and your customers were in the middle of an experience that is part of your topic. Then, relive what you thought, remember what you said, and write down what was going on in your heart and head.

The resulting Conversational Catchphrases will describe what happened in a natural, organic voice that will resonate with people because they'll sense it is authentic. Feature these exclamations in your ads, website copy, marketing material, and programs, and people will seek out your advice, buy your products, or at least be open to hearing more because they'll sense you're a kindred spirit who's been there, done that.

Step 1. Ask yourself, What do current and prospective customers say when dealing with *my* situation? What would I tell myself if this were happening to me? What dilemma does my product solve? How do people feel when dealing with this?

Step 2. Now, ask yourself, What do people think about issues associated with my topic, but *wouldn't dare say out loud*? Capture the "underground" catchphrases that people feel, but may not readily admit. This can uncover unexpressed concerns people are desperate to know more about.

Step 3. Anticipate what people would like to say when this challenge was successfully resolved. Capture those "Eureka" and "At last" exclamations of joy that would cause a prospective customer to think, "I'll have what they're having."

Step 4. Review the catchphrases you've written down to see which ones elicit a heartfelt "Yes" or "That's exactly how I feel" response. If you use one of those for your title or slogan or feature it in your product or program description, people will immediately connect with it because it expresses how they already feel, want to feel, or don't want to feel about this subject.

5

Create Tell 'n Sell Introductions with the Valley Girl Technique

I know that you believe you understand what you think I said,
but I'm not sure you realize that what you heard is not
what I meant.

ROBERT MCCLOSKEY

I came up with this technique when I was on a speaking tour in Denver, with my teenage sons. We had a free night so we asked our hotel concierge for suggestions on where we could go for a fun night out. He took one look at Tom and Andrew and said, "You've got to go to D & B's."

We were from Maui at the time and had no idea what he was talking about. I asked, "What's D & B's?"

He thought for a moment, and then, instead of explaining that it stood for "Dave and Buster's," he grinned and said, "It's like . . . Chuck E. Cheese's for adults."

Perfect! Seven words and we understood exactly what it was and were eager to go there. By comparing something we didn't know to something we knew and liked, he "told and sold" that place in one succinct sound bite. They should have put him on commission.

What do you say when people ask, "What do you do?"

Do you have a clear, concise, and compelling "Tell 'n Sell" elevator introduction for yourself, your company, creation, cause, or campaign? Even if we don't like the "What do you do?" question, we might as well get used to it because it's never going away. When people meet us for the first time, they have no context for us. Asking what we do is simply their way of trying to get a handle on who we are so they have a hook on which to hang a conversation. Instead of dreading that question, it's smart to invest the time to create an intriguing response that motivates people to want to know more. View it as a carte blanche opportunity to establish a favorable first impression for you and your services, product, or company.

MAKE THEM UNDERSTAND AND MAKE THEM EAGER

You never really understand a person until you climb into his skin and walk around in it.
HARPER LEE

You may be thinking, "Okay, but what does this have to do with Valley Girls?" Have you ever been to Southern California? If so, you may have encountered teenage girls from the San Fernando Valley who, when asked to explain something, tilt their head to the side, shuffle their feet, put their index finger on their cheek, and twist it back and forth while saying, "It's *like* . . . you know."

To Valley Girl your idea, product, or business, simply ask yourself, What is this *like* . . . with a twist? What movie is it like . . . with a twist? What person is it like . . . with a twist? What song is it like . . . with a twist? What book is it like . . . with a twist?

When people hear about your idea or invention for the first time, they don't have any framework for it. The Valley Girl technique links something unfamiliar (you or your project) to something they are familiar with and fond of. When done well, this technique gives people an instant "Aha!" Something obscure becomes clear.

For example, the insurance giant State Farm has a slogan that links their organization to something everyone wants. Their purpose was to imprint the impression their company could be turned to and trusted in trying times. That raises the question, "To whom do we turn in trying times?" Well, if we need help in a hurry, we might turn to our neighbors for help and support. This comparison— "*Like* a good neighbor, State Farm is there"—reinforces the comforting notion you can count on State Farm in times of need.

VALLEY GIRL A FAMOUS PERSON

*I always wanted to be someone, but I should
have been more specific.*
LILY TOMLIN AND JANE WAGNER

Dale Irvin (www.daleirvin.com) is a funny man who gets paid to emcee conferences, but he does much more than that. He attends as many sessions as possible and takes notes on all the proceedings. Then, during general assemblies, he offers humorous observations about conference goings-on. Because he's so good at what he does, Dale has attendees rolling in the aisles with his comic insights. A bonus is that he creates a community of the meeting participants because they're laughing at—and sharing and creating—common memories.

You can imagine Dale's dilemma. As is true for many of us, his work isn't easy to describe. It's a challenge to sum up all the nuances of what we do in a few words.

Dale had been calling himself a "professional summarizer," but that didn't do justice to his comedic brilliance. Then, a meeting planner who was thrilled with his work gave him the perfect Tell 'n

Sell summary that captured the essence of his service. She said, "What Billy Crystal does for the Academy Awards, you did for our convention."

To do this, ask yourself, Who is well-known for doing what I do in another profession—someone my target audience is familiar with? What are the characteristics of my job and who is famous for doing something similar in another industry? Who else operates like I do in a different setting? Comparing yourself to that person can provide a type of verbal shorthand that helps people "get" and "want" what you do because you're linking your work to something they relate to and respect. Fill in the blanks and create your own variation of this sentence by combining *their* name or label with *your* name or label as in "What _____ does for _____, I do for you."

Amy Krouse Rosenthal wanted to share ideas on how to be a loving mother even when juggling many responsibilities. Her premise was, in the first few months of life, babies don't understand language so they respond more to our temperament. If we are frenzied, frazzled, and uptight, our baby will probably be frenzied, frazzled, and uptight. If, on the other hand, we are calm, peaceful, and tranquil, our baby is more likely to be calm, peaceful, and tranquil.

It took me a paragraph to explain that concept. If we want to Valley Girl her philosophy, we simply ask, "Who is an international figure known for being calm, peaceful, and tranquil?" Well, there's Mother Teresa. Gandhi. How about the Dalai Lama? Hmm . . . that has potential. Let's run that name through the alphabet to see what we come up with. Dalai Aama, Dalai Bama, Dalai Cama, and in a little bit, you get . . . *Dalai Mama!* That's it. Two words and we know exactly what she's talking about.

The Cleveland Clinic has been consistently rated one of the best hospitals in the country; however, they were having a hard time overcoming the misperception that Cleveland is a "medical backwater" and couldn't possibly be the home of a world-class medical facility. They asked themselves, What other industry is well-known for having rankings and what are they called? From there, it was a short creative leap to designing an ad that featured a huge headline saying, "Imagine staying atop the bestseller list every week since 1995."

That headline is surrounded by a lot of white space so it stands out. The bottom third of the ad says, "The Cleveland Clinic Heart Center has been ranked #1 in the nation by *U.S. News & World Report* for 11 consecutive years. If you need heart care, we're here to help." That's a brilliant demonstration of how the Valley Girl technique can lend your organization credibility by comparing it to something that is already credible.

VALLEY GIRL A WELL-KNOWN MOVIE

Never judge a book by its movie.
J. W. EAGAN

Contrary to what Eagan said, sometimes we can create an intriguing Tell 'n Sell intro by judging how our work compares to popular books and movies.

A writers conference attendee named Wally uses a sonar device to "douse" for whales. Once he locates a pod, he lowers the device into the ocean to record their sounds. He has studied their language and claims to be able to communicate with the whales.

The challenge was, how could Wally pitch this rather esoteric topic to publishers without coming across like he was one taco short of a combination platter? He didn't have a degree in marine biology and wasn't on the staff of a recognized research organization, so he was having a tough time earning respect for his expertise. How could he crystallize his lifetime work into a compelling sound bite that established credibility and intrigue?

We Valley Girled his topic. What was a movie that featured someone who could talk to animals? How about Eddie Murphy in *Dr. Doolittle*? Well, that wouldn't work because that was a comedy and Wally's purpose was to gain respect for his work. Remember, POP! titles need to be purposeful. Comparing himself to a comedic actor would not position him favorably with his target audience—editors.

So, we kept listing movies that featured characters who could communicate with animals. Wait a minute. How about the movie *The Horse Whisperer*? That was it. Wally started introducing himself as *The Whale Whisperer*. That succinct and evocative sound bite invariably elicited an intrigued "Hmm . . . tell me more."

It's easy to find a list of movies for your elevator intro. Just visit www.imdb.com to access the Internet Movie Database. How much simpler could it be?

VALLEY GIRL A BESTSELLING BOOK

Books take us to places we didn't even suspect existed.
MAUREEN CORRIGAN

Valley Girling your project to a bestselling book can give you a title, tagline, or intro that delights people because it's unexpectedly clever.

A friend of mine is a beautiful woman in her fifties who heads up a large trade association. She's also a grandmother, single, and dating. She wanted to write about her eclectic experiences juggling these different personal and professional roles. She already had an intriguing title, *Hell on Heels*, for her book that contained brief, humorous, self-contained vignettes about what it was like to be running a board meeting one hour and running to meet someone she "winked at" on Match.com the next. Now she needed to design a response to that all-important question, "What's your book about?"

I kept asking her, "What's your book like? What's it *like*?" Finally, she blurted out, "It's like Bridget Jones's mother's diary." To answer your question, she can't use that as a title because she didn't author the book *Bridget Jones's Diary*, but she can use that Tell 'n Sell analogy when pitching the book so agents quickly grasp its style and tone.

VALLEY GIRL A POPULAR SONG

"What If My Ship Comes In and I'm at the Airport?"
SONG TITLE IN KATHI KAMEN GOLDMARK'S BOOK
AND MY SHOES KEEP WALKING BACK TO YOU

Another way to create an enticing Tell 'n Sell intro or title is to pull out your list of Core Words and start thinking of all the songs you know that contain those words. Fortunately, you can also go to www.lyricsfree.com, enter your Core Words one at a time, and come up with a list of song titles containing your key phrases.

Since song titles and lyrics are usually copyrighted, you won't want to use them verbatim. Substitute your own creative twist to produce an ear-grabbing introduction or title. To do this, replace a key word in the song title with an Alphabetized or Spell Chuck version of one of your Core Words. For example, a computer expert in Washington, DC, who specializes in fixing Macintosh computers, promises around-the-clock service, even if that means visiting your house late at night if your computer decides to crash just when you need to print out your important paper or essay. Do any of you Baby Boomers remember a famous song by Bobby Darrin featuring the word "Mac?" His clever business name—*Mac the Night*.

Doug Morris, a client of mine, is an expert on sprawl (the spread of drive-everywhere-in-a-car suburbs that lack connected communities). This is an important topic, but Doug knows it doesn't sound very exciting. His subject may have elicited the dreaded "So?"

Doug speaks at environmental conferences and is often interviewed by the media (most recently C-SPAN) to explain how sprawl is harming America. His premise is, if we drive everywhere, we don't get to know our neighbors. Which means they become strangers. And of course, we're not supposed to talk to strangers. And if we don't talk to them, we don't feel connected with them. Even though we're surrounded by people, we feel increasingly isolated and alienated, which can lead to antagonism, even violence.

Doug was having a hard time generating interest in this vital subject, so we Alphabetized his Core Words to create proprietary sound bites that helped his message POP! If you run the word *sprawl* through the alphabet, you come up with brawl. Well, *Sprawl Brawl* is a good name for the increasing incivility and road rage. Then there's *Sprawl Crawl*, which perfectly describes the expansion of cookie-cutter homes. How about *Sprawl Mall* for today's version of a shopping-center gathering place, except we don't know anyone there and there are no long-time mom and pop owners, which only increases our feeling of anonymity and alienation? Alphabetizing helped him craft more interesting intellectual capital.

Next, we Valley Girled popular songs. Sprawl is a little-used word so we didn't think there'd be any top forty hits about it. What's a more common word that sounds like *sprawl*? How about *small*? There are a lot of songs with *small* in them. The next thing we knew, we were both humming the Disney classic "It's a Small World After All." One little adjustment morphed that into a title that helped Doug land a deal with a respected publisher. *It's a Sprawl Word After All.* Tah-dah!

That's another benefit of this technique. By linking your unpublished or unproduced product to a "done deal," you make it real. By connecting your new product to a proven product, their established reputation rubs off on you. You're turning something speculative into something substantive. Fame by proxy.

HOW TO USE THE VALLEY GIRL TECHNIQUE

The only real risk is the risk of thinking too small.
FRANCES MOORE LAPPÉ

Ready to develop a Tell 'n Sell elevator intro that "has them at hello"? Ready to develop a sound-bite slogan that succinctly explains what you have to offer in a way that people get it and want it?

Step 1. Ask yourself, Who is well-known for doing what I do—in another context? Who exemplifies the benefits of my product? Who is my "twin" in another industry? Write down the names that occur to you.

Step 2. Now, take each of your Core Words and enter them into www.imdb.com to generate a list of movie titles that include phrases relevant to your cause or campaign. Write down movie titles that look promising, even if you're not sure right now how you can use them for comparison or incorporate them into your marketing material.

Step 3. Take each of your Core Words and enter them, one at a time, into the search engine at your favorite online bookstore (www.amazon.com, www.barnesandnoble.com). Write down the names of books that catch your eye and ear.

Step 4. Take each of your Core Words and check them with www.lyricsfree.com to find song titles or memorable lyrics that resonate with you and that could be relevant to your target audience. Write down any that "sing" to you and that might provide a clever variation on your theme that will delight your readers or listeners.

Step 5. Now, review your notes. What phrases caught your attention? Could you make slight adjustments to any of the movie, book, or song titles so you have a unique twist on a familiar phrase? Play with this phrase. My _____ (screenplay? invention? product?) is like _____ with _____. For example, the Hollywood high-concept pitch for the movie *Jaws* could be "My screenplay is like *Moby Dick* . . . with a shark" or "A fish . . . with an attitude."

Step 6. Beware of the "cheese factor." Overly cute elevator intros can be a turn-off. Remember the fourth question on your W9 Form, "Who is your target audience?" If you're networking in a room of executives, addressing your board of directors, or being interviewed by the *Wall Street Journal*, you could seriously harm your credibility if you trot out a groaner. You want to gain respect, not contempt.

The Valley Girl technique can broaden your scope and help you develop a Tell 'n Sell elevator introduction (notice I didn't say speech—who wants to listen to a speech?) that pleasantly surprises people with its novelty. By accessing famous movie, song, or book titles and names of celebrities, you are stretching your basis of comparison and accessing thousands of options. Instead of thinking small and only calling upon what you know, you are thinking big. As a result, you're more likely to arrive at a concept that has broad appeal, universal meaning, and instant recognition . . . all at the same time.

6

Increase Likability with Laugh Lines

I learned that when I made people laugh, they liked me.
This is a lesson I'll never forget.
ART BUCHWALD

Southwest Airlines is famous for its quick-witted pilots and flight attendants. In that intensely competitive industry, they believe it helps endear them to the many road warriors who rack up tens of thousands of air miles every year. Although staff members make sure to steer clear of any jokes about security, fear of flying, or maintenance problems, everything else is fair game. If, for example, they have a bumpy landing, the pilot is likely to come on the intercom and say, "Folks, contrary to popular belief, that wasn't the captain's fault. That wasn't even the first officer's fault. That was what we call the 'asphalt.'"

As Art Buchwald sagely pointed out, anytime we elicit a laugh, people are more likely to like us and whatever it is we're offering.

You may be thinking, I agree with the power of humor, but I'm not naturally funny. Don't worry; other people are. Start keeping your eyes and ears open and you'll find plenty of humor around to punch up your material. In fact, if you want be a HUMORiginal, you can follow the advice given to brides at their wedding and include *something old*, *something new*, *something borrowed*, and *something blue*.

USE OLD HUMOR

If you can laugh at it, you can live with it.
Erma Bombeck

Do you have any old family stories—something amusing that happened around the dinner table or while on a vacation? It may not have been funny at the time, but you all laugh about it now?

My sons and I were discussing weekend plans while eating dinner. Tom seemed rather distracted. I asked, "Are you listening to me?" "Sure, Mom," he said innocently. "You have my *undevoted* attention."

If you're conducting an employee orientation tomorrow, you could tell that story and then segue into, "I know listening to all these rules and regulations isn't exactly scintillating and you might be tempted to study the inside of your eyelids. I'm hoping you'll give me your *undivided* attention for the next ten minutes so you'll understand how these procedures affect you on the job."

USE NEW HUMOR

Life abounds in comedy if you just look around.
Mel Brooks

The next time you watch a TV sitcom or late-night talk show, write down whatever makes you laugh. A good rule of thumb is, if it makes you laugh, it will probably make other people laugh. Review those one-liners after the program and select one that is relevant to incorporate into your next web article, sales pitch, or introduction.

Remember to attribute the original line to its source and then share your variation on their theme.

For example, if you're a *Friends* fan, you may remember the episode in which Phoebe, the self-described blond ditz who sings "Smelly Cat," was complaining nonstop about her brother. Joey couldn't stand it anymore and interrupted her with, "Phoebe, have you told your brother how you feel?" "Yes," Phoebe replied, looking rather offended. Then, hanging her head, she confessed, "Well, not *out loud.*"

If you are a therapist or psychologist who counsels couples, you could share this vignette in a presentation or during a media interview and then ask, "Are you unhappy with how someone is treating you? Are you telling that person off—in your mind? Are you complaining to everyone else how upset you are—but not bringing it to the attention of the person who's responsible?"

See how starting off with the story about Phoebe engages people from the start because it's a more innovative way to broach this subject? Instead of blah, blah, blah rhetoric that comes across as a lecture (such as, "It's important to let people know when we don't like how they're behaving."), this humorous anecdote has them listening and learning.

USE BORROWED HUMOR (WITH ATTRIBUTION)

I refuse to answer that question on the grounds that I don't know the answer.
DOUGLAS ADAMS

Have you ever been asked a question and your brain went blank? From now on, instead of just standing there tongue-tied, you could share the above quip . . . and give credit to Douglas Adams. We don't have to be quick on our verbal feet as long as we have a reper-toire of clever comebacks to call upon when the situation warrants.

Get out your list of Core Words and check the index of one of Judy Brown's fabulous resources, *Joke Soup* or *Joke Stew*. I like her books because they feature one-liners from current comedians such as Steven Wright, Jay Leno, Robin Williams, and Judy Tenuta. You can also type in "joke" to your favorite search engine and a variety of joke dictionaries and websites will appear. It is okay to use one-liners, *as long as you do it sparingly and reference the source*. If a joke or funny story is longer than a couple of sentences or if you want to feature a comedian's one-liner in a commercial or ad campaign, it is necessary to get permission before you use that person's intellectual capital.

When you use a quip and then segue into how that relates to your idea or invention, that's called a "hook and hinge." The joke hooks people's interest, and then you hinge the punch line onto how it's relevant to your point or product.

For example, if you are a tax preparer whose work schedule is wide open in February and jam-packed in March and April, you might want to send an e-mail blast to your client list suggesting they file early instead of waiting until the last minute when they might not be able to get an appointment. Instead of warning them not to put this off (which could come across as scolding), you could "hook" 'em with Judy Tenuta's tongue-in-cheek line, "My parents always told me I wouldn't amount to anything because I procrastinated so much. I told them, 'Just you wait.'" Then hinge with "Have you been procrastinating on your taxes because you've been so busy? Have you been waiting to collect all the proper forms and paper-work? Let us help. Call now and we can simplify the process."

You get the idea. This fresh approach might be enough incentive for your clients to e-mail or call to schedule an appointment instead of continuing to put it off.

If you're like most people, you receive joke lists that make the rounds of the Internet. From now on, don't immediately delete them.

Read them with a purpose in mind. Do any of them relate to your product, business, or service? Could you borrow one of those lines (with attribution) and include it in your message to make it POP!?

These next suggestions play off a joke list that showed up in my inbox. If you are selling:

- upholstery repair, perhaps your slogan could be, "Is your furniture fully recovered?"
- security systems, your ad could say, "Alarmed? You should be."
- distinctive wines, perhaps you could herald your "Best Cellar."
- your inventory at a deep discount, you could put up a huge banner saying, "50% off—and that's just the half of it."

Please note: It is not appropriate or smart to base website copy or marketing collateral on something you got from the Internet because it is already ubiquitous . . . and it could belong to someone else. If it has been making the web rounds, chances are thousands, if not millions, of people have seen it already. That would make your material and campaign derivative—and you want to be creative, not a copycat.

USE SOMETHING BLUE (NOT!)

A thing is funny when—in some way that is not actually offensive or frightening—it upsets the established order. Every joke is a tiny revolution.
GEORGE ORWELL

I'm not recommending you use blue humor (e.g., coarse language, offensive slang, or politically incorrect jokes). I'm recommending you use *out-of-the-blue* humor. If someone says something out of the blue that makes you laugh out loud, remember it will probably make other people laugh out loud too. You've just been given a gift. Figure out how to weave it into your marketing message. What point could it illustrate?

Years ago, Karl Haas, he of the terrific deep bass voice and host of the popular NPR program *Adventures in Good Music*, came to town to present an evening program featuring his behind-the-scenes insights about classical music. The packed crowd eagerly awaited this opportunity to see him in person. Following an eloquent introduction, out walked Karl Haas. The audience gasped. Much to their surprise, their radio hero was about five feet nothing. Haas was obviously accustomed to this reaction and had prepared a riposte. With a twinkle in his eye, he leaned out toward the group and said, "I didn't know what you looked like either!" Bravo.

If you had been in that audience and were thinking like a HUMORiginal, you would have immediately asked yourself, "How can I use that?" If you were a political consultant, you could share that story with clients and point out how Haas had successfully defused a sensitive issue by preparing an amusing remark that addressed the "elephant in the room." You could then ask what challenging questions might come up during their public appearances or media interviews. Next you could prepare and rehearse appropriate responses so they're not caught off guard and can handle those situations with poise rather than panic.

Make sure your humor is appropriate *before* breaking it out in public. Comedy is subjective, so it's in your best interests to have a trial run before risking your good will or your organization's reputation on something your target audience finds offensive. Simply ask a few people what they think of your proposed anecdote, or run your one-liner by your colleagues to get their reactions as to whether this is wise or ill-advised.

Risky humor can pay off, as long as you calculate the possible consequences in advance and determine that the payoffs outweigh the drawbacks. A friend told me about a famous nail salon in Texas.

The inspired name? *Tex's Chainsaw Manicure*. Some people may not appreciate that name and may take their business elsewhere. On the other hand (so to speak), that creative name has attracted national press and many loyal fans.

MAKE THE LAUGHTER LEAD TO SOMETHING PURPOSEFUL

It has always surprised me how little attention philosophers have paid to humor since it is a more significant process of mind than reason. Reason can only sort out perceptions; humor is involved in changing them.

EDWARD DE BONO

It's great to get a guffaw, but it's important to make sure your target audience remembers the name of your product that was featured in the material that made them laugh. Did the laughs translate into some type of sale? Did it get your proposal approved? Did it take the tension out of a controversy and help turn a no into a yes? Did it change your customers' perception of you or your cause or campaign for the better?

Do you remember the incident at the 2004 Super Bowl when Janet Jackson had a "wardrobe malfunction" when Justin Timberlake "mistakenly" ripped off the top of her outfit? An enterprising journalist capitalized on that term in his article about race car driver Dale Earnhardt Jr. being fined $10,000 for uttering a swear word in the victory lane after winning the Talladega 500. The article's title? *Vocabulary Malfunction*.

Years ago, I read about a bakery owner who was beleaguered with requests for the recipe for her popular bread. She finally posted a sign that said, "Our secret recipe for our world-famous bread will be provided on a 'knead to know' basis only." That amusing sign gave her a way to politely refuse requests for her closely guarded recipe without alienating her customers.

LAUGH AT YOURSELF BEFORE THEY CAN LAUGH AT YOU

> *Perhaps one has to become very old before one learns*
> *how to be amused rather than offended.*
> PEARL S. BUCK

Why wait? Why not learn now? Celebrities have long known the power of poking fun at themselves before others can poke fun at them. They realize the best way to take the sting out of peoples' barbs is to beat them to the punch line.

Jon Stewart (of TV's *Daily Show* fame) did an excellent job of doing this when he hosted the Academy Awards. Stewart anticipated a cool reception from the Hollywood audience and mocked his last-choice status by skewering himself with, "Tonight is the night we celebrate excellence in film, with me, the fourth male lead from *Death to Smoochy*." This was a classic "poke fun at yourself before other people do" gambit that accomplished its goal of winning over the audience.

What's that got to do with you? Will you be speaking to a group that is questioning your credentials? Are you hosting an event in which participants are likely to have their mental arms crossed? Instead of taking umbrage at their lack of respect, the question is, how can you show humility and humor so they're laughing *with* you instead of *at* you?

Saddled with a challenging call sign (SUX), the Sioux City airport was on the verge of asking the FAA for permission to change its name. In a bold move, they decided to have fun with the name instead of being embarrassed by it. Their new marketing campaign,

"FlyingSux," has produced so much free press that airlines have actually added flights into Sioux City. As a bonus, "Fly SUX" T-shirts and caps have become a popular novelty item and cash registers are kept busy ringing up sales.

HOW TO USE THE LAUGH LINES TECHNIQUE

I'm always looking for something to engage my imagination and take me on a little voyage. I just want a new topic in my life.
STEVE MARTIN

Step 1. Become a HUMORiginal by keeping your antennae up for amusing anecdotes. When somebody says or does something that tickles your funny bone, write it down and toss it into a file that is labeled with your project title.

Step 2. When you watch TV shows or movies, pay attention to what makes you laugh. Take the time to write it down and label it with the point of what happened or with a couple key words that relate to your cause, creation, or campaign.

Step 3. Remember the advice given to brides. Plumb your past to see if you might have any "old" anecdotes in your history that could provide an amusing, heartwarming illustration to one of your points. "Borrow" one-liners from online joke lists (after giving credit to the originator) to hook and hinge your topic to capture and keep your audience's attention. Introduce "new" quips from current comedians and then segue into your subject. Capitalize on "out-of-the-blue" situations that have you and others laughing out loud by writing down what happened so you can use it later.

Step 4. When you are preparing to speak or write, delve into your files to see if you've stashed away just the right one-liner or anecdote that will elicit a chuckle and a warm response that wins people over to what you're offering.

7

Don't Repeat Clichés, Rearrange Clichés

Avoid clichés like the plague.
SAMUEL GOLDWYN

Phil Jackson, former coach of the Chicago Bulls basketball team, once told star player Michael Jordan to stop hogging the ball. He said, "You need to start passing the ball to open players. Remember, Michael, there's no 'I' in team."

Jordan replied with a twinkle in his eyes, "Yeah, but there is in win."

Yes! Next time you're tempted to trot out a trite truism, turn it on its head as Michael did and pleasantly surprise your audience.

Trotting out tired expressions (such as, "It's nice to be important, but it's more important to be nice") sends the message that we don't have anything new to add to the conversation. I'm not saying these sentiments aren't true; they're just not new. They elicit a "So what?" response and many people will roll their eyes and tune out.

You don't have to avoid clichés altogether. Just add your own unique twist instead of repeating them verbatim. Substituting something unexpected for something expected startles people out of autopilot mode and pleasantly surprises them with your originality.

TURN EYE-ROLLERS INTO EYE-OPENERS

Great minds like a think.
THE ECONOMIST

The above tagline for the *Economist* is brilliant. It turns a platitude into a powerful and purposeful slogan that perfectly captures the tone of the magazine while complimenting its customers' intelligence. That's why it's included in my POP! Hall of Fame. (See all ten winners at the end of the book.)

Two former executives opened a dog-walking business that combined their love of fitness and animals. Carol and Leslie were both marathoners, so they took their canine clients for long runs in the country instead of simply heading to the "bark park." When they keyed in their Core Words to their favorite search engine, up popped literally hundreds of references. Dog magazines, dog stores, dog shows, dog kennels, and more. They read the buffet of ideas and designed a brochure for their business that never fails to get a laugh, a referral, or a follow-up call.

Their name and slogan? *DogOn Fitness*: "We're more than just a walk around the block!"

Imagine you are writing descriptive copy for your website, an article for an internal newsletter, or an op-ed for a local newspaper. Your goal is to spice it up so it stands out. Take your Core Words and go to www.clichesite.com. Enter each word into the search engine and up will come a variety of clichés with your words. Write down the aphorisms that appeal to you, and let the wordplay begin.

For example, a participant in one of my POP! presentations was asked to write an article for her professional association's trade journal about the importance of using plain English instead of bureaucratic gobbledygook. She could have titled that article something straightforward like "The Importance of Direct Communication."

Yawn. Instead, she called it *No Plain, No Gain*. Her editor called to thank her, delighted with her inventive title and her fresh information on how to produce "no-doze prose."

CUT OUT THE PLATITUDES

Drama is life with the dull bits cut out.
ALFRED HITCHCOCK

POP! is an elevator pitch with the dull parts cut out. A client told me, "Your suggestion to rearrange clichés to make them our own is similar to what I do as a jazz pianist. When I want to improvise, I start by playing the song's standard chords and then riff off those to create my own unique melody and new musical combinations. It seems you're recommending we do something similar with our Core Words. By riffing off common clichés we can create our own unique message and never-before-heard language combinations."

He was right. Riffing off a well-known saying can jazz up our communication and turn something dull into something delightful.

Please note the cliché or quote doesn't actually have to contain one of your Core Words. Cliché and quote dictionaries are often arranged in alphabetical order. If your Core Word starts with I, just look up all the clichés under the *I* section and substitute your word or a synonym in the appropriate spot. For example, you might see this classic quote, "I think, therefore I am." Substitute a product name and you get, "I think, therefore iPod," or fill in a company name and you have, "I think, therefore IBM."

NO MORE BUSINESS AS USUAL

Discovery is said to be an accident meeting a prepared mind.
ALBERT SZENT-GYORGYI

Believe it or not, I read cliché dictionaries and quote books for fun. (Just call me a party animal.) You can develop a talent for conjuring clever plays on words by taking a cliché dictionary to lunch one day this week. Have a pencil in hand and start on page one. Read through each cliché, replacing key words with alliterative substitutions to see if you can turn an old saying into a new slogan for your business so it gets the attention it deserves.

Professional speaker Michael David Hoffman offers a program for salespeople on how to avoid aggressive body language and off-putting openings called, "You Lost Me at Hello." Humorist Loretta Laroche titled her latest book, *Squeeze the Day: 365 Ways to Bring More Joy and Juice into Your Life*. A baker might want to put a sign in her window advertising her fresh bread, "Give Yeast a Chance." A wine shop could offer a wine-tasting called "Life is a Cabernet." A financial expert who specializes in advising newlywed couples could produce an e-book titled, *Till Debt Do Us Part*. A local arts-and-craft store is called Knit Happens. A car-repair shop specializing in lube jobs and brake repair displays a banner that says, "Your squeaky wheel gets our grease." A massage therapist introduced herself at a networking function with this motto, "I rub people the right way." See how easy this is? Just start off a cliché the old way . . . and finish it in a new way.

If you're opening a bicycle shop that specializes in mountain bike and road racing, answer the questions in Chapter 2 and develop your W9 Form to describe your inventory and services. Enter your Core Words (such as, "tires, spokes, race, gears, sweat") into your cliché dictionary, which could trigger *Blood, Sweat, and Gears*, a great name for your shop or a smile-inducing headline for an ad.

Patti Eyres, a lawyer who delivers corporate keynotes on e-mail use and abuse, changed her title, "Everything You Need to Know About E-mail—But Didn't Know to Ask" to "Is Your E-mail a Pain in the Net?" which resulted in Patti booking ten new keynote presentations almost immediately.

UNFREEZE YOUR CREATIVITY

You can sit there, tense and worried, freezing the creative
energies, or you can start writing something, perhaps
something silly. It doesn't matter what. In five or
ten minutes, the imagination will heat, the tightness
will fade, and a certain spirit and rhythm will take over.

LEONARD BERNSTEIN

Allen Stam consults with companies on how they can maximize profits from their trade-show exhibits. He practices what he teaches by reinforcing his slogan "Take Your Booth by the Horns" with clever merchandise that keeps him POP! of Mind with clients. He passes out pens that have their top shaped like the business end of a Texas longhorn.

I admit it. I'm a *USA Today* and *Washington Post* junkie. My morning ritual is to take my dog, Murphy, out for a walk around the lake and then return to my favorite chair by the window, cup of coffee in one hand, morning papers in the other.

The reporters and editors at both of these newspapers are absolutely brilliant with their headlines. Not a day goes by, and that is not an exaggeration, that I don't laugh out loud at some clever play on words. For example, in a recent issue, the *Washington Post* had a story by staff writer William Booth about director David Lynch (of *Blue Velvet* fame), who is now sponsoring Transcendental Meditation universities based on the teachings of Maharishi Mahesh Yogi (the Beatles' former guru). The headline? "Yogi Bearer." But it doesn't stop there. A subheading on the next page that introduces the purpose of repeating a mantra is "More than a Chant Encounter."

Not to be outdone, business writer Steven Pearlstein wrote about the terror some A-types were feeling at the prospect of not having access to their BlackBerries due to pending litigation. What was the title of his article that discussed the dangers of not protecting proprietary technology? "Big Firms Caught with Their Patents Down." This same issue featured a book review by Carolyn See about a new biography written by Linda Bird Francke called *On the Road with Francis of Assisi*. The title of See's review? "A Saint for Sore Eyes."

Hats off to the headline writers at the *Washington Post* for their brilliant ability to invent intriguing, relevant titles that pull readers in. Many mornings I'll be in a rush and about to put the paper aside when one of their evocative headlines captivates me and, the next thing I know, I'm reading another article.

A friend told me about a headline in the *Wall Street Journal* that caught her attention. The article described an interesting development in the airline industry. Rather than turning in their frequent-flier miles for more flights (a win for the carriers), customers were hoarding their miles in the hopes of exchanging them for high-dollar items such as flat-panel TVs and diamond earrings. The name of the article? "Now Hoarding."

You may be thinking, That sounds like a lot of work. Ask yourself, Is it worth an hour of my time to create a title and tagline that could drive thousands of dollars of revenue? Is it worth the effort to develop an intriguing intro that captures people's interest every time it's heard? Creating clever names and slogans is a front-loaded process, but it can pay dividends for years to come.

HOW TO USE THE REARRANGE CLICHÉ TECHNIQUE

How do I work? I grope.
ALBERT EINSTEIN

Ready to try this technique for your project? Please bring out your W9 Form because you're going to use your Core Words to find relevant clichés for your topic or project.

Step 1. Enter the word *cliché* into your favorite search engine. It will list a variety of cliché dictionary websites. Select the one that appeals to you (my favorite is www.clichesite.com).

Step 2. Key in your Core Words, one at a time. Scan the options, writing down any that elicit a visceral reaction from you. If they're intriguing, profound, funny . . . write them down!

Step 3. Now, replace or riff off the key words in that cliché. Switch the key nouns or verbs to make a play on words.

For example, I was a guest on a Toronto TV talk show the same day songbird Shania Twain was visiting. The city was thrilled to have her back in town (she's a Canadian native), but her public appearance was cancelled due to an unexpected storm. The headline in the paper the next morning described the thousands of disappointed fans who didn't get to see their hometown hero. I bet you can come up with the headline that made me laugh out loud. Take Shania's last name and think of a cliché that contains that word. Factor in that her fans didn't get to meet her as hoped, reverse the key words and you get "Never Shall Meet the Twain."

Step 4. Keep experimenting. As the saying goes, If at first you don't succeed, you're about average. You might immediately compose an uncommon twist on a cliché that makes your new slogan POP!, or it might take a while to crystallize a new saying that will help your product stand out. Remember, if groping was good enough for Einstein, it ought to be good enough for us.

Ready to learn how to help people picture your product in their mind, which moves them closer to wanting it for their own? On to the next chapter.

8

Aflac Your Topic So They *See* What You're *Saying*

The soul never thinks without a mental picture.
ARISTOTLE

PR expert Marilynn Mobley, who has an excellent blog on the topic of relevance (www.remainrelevant.blogspot.com), recently told me about a startling study that was done with preschoolers. When asked what sounds animals made, they gave the usual answers: sheep—*baa*, cows—*moo*, horses—*neigh*, and so on. When asked what sound ducks made, they said, "Aflac!"

Wow. Talk about a brand owning mindshare.

Let's examine what happened. This insurance company faced a daunting challenge. Their name was nonsensical. What is an Aflac? People know what a Mustang is. They know what a landscape architect does. But when your name is a string of letters that stands for something meaningful (and known) only to you, it's hard for people to feel warm and fuzzy about it. Why would people want to give their money to a firm when they don't even know what its name means?

Aflac's brilliant advertising team took a name that was difficult to relate to and tied their grouping of five letters to something people could see and hear. What does Aflac sound like? What does it look like? Well, with a little stretch, it looks and sounds like a duck, ergo, Aflac=duck. Because of their TV commercials and print ads featuring a duck quacking, "Aflac," people now associate that abstract business name with an adorable animal, which put that insurance company on the mental map of millions of Americans. Aflac now has favorable name recognition, one of the first steps to becoming a viable option for consumers.

Another insurance company did the same thing, with similar success. What do the letters GEICO mean to you? As a series of letters, nothing. However, thanks to their clever commercials, you probably picture a cute gecko that you now associate with GEICO insurance. Instead of perceiving them to be a huge anonymous conglomerate with no "soul," you now *picture* this amusing creature that elicits amusement (a warm emotion) and you are more favorably predisposed to consider them as an option.

WHEN PEOPLE SEE IT, THEY GET IT

Necessity is the mother of invention.
PLATO

If necessity is the mother of invention, visualization is the father. Does your business or product have a nonsensical name? If your organization's name is a string of letters or a combination of words that don't relate to anything in real life (for example, Arescom, Textran, B.R.N.), you may be losing potential customers.

Why? As discussed in previous chapters, we want people to remember our name; therefore, they must be able to relate to it. If they read or hear our name and slogan and it doesn't mean anything to them, why should they care? If our name is just a collection of letters, it doesn't produce an image in their mind. That means they haven't visually grasped it, which means they're not imprinting it.

And if they're not imprinting your name, how can they recommend you to a colleague or find your product in the store? What's worse, many people have averse reactions to weird-sounding names and may avoid the company altogether.

The beauty of the Aflac technique, named in honor of the company that so successfully models the power of this concept, is that it moves people from a logical frame of mind to an emotional frame of mind. When a new idea or term is introduced to people, their minds try to make sense of it by associating it to something they already know. You can expedite this process by comparing and connecting the unknown item to something it is like in the real world. Aaaahhh. All of a sudden, it makes sense. They *see* the connection. They often either think or say out loud, "I see now" or "I get it." That's why this is called the "I see, I get" approach.

When you tell people your business name or slogan, do they get it? Can they see it? When you introduce your idea, can people picture what you're talking about in their mind? Can they link it to something visual in the real world? If so, great. If not, it would help to ask yourself, What is my product or business name? What else sounds like that that people are familiar with? What is my idea? What is that like in the real world that people could relate to?

One of the most dramatic examples of the power of "Aflacing" your idea so that people can see it and be moved by it was modeled by Hillary Clinton when she ended her presidential campaign and threw her support to Senator Barack Obama. As Dana Milbank said in a June 8, 2008, *Washington Post* column, "During the campaign, her opponent owned the lofty rhetoric. But on the day she conceded defeat, it was Hillary Clinton's words that soared, 'As we gather here today, the fiftieth woman to leave this Earth is orbiting overhead. If we can blast fifty women into space, we will someday launch a woman into the White House. Although we weren't able to shatter that highest, hardest glass ceiling this time, thanks to you, it's got about eighteen million cracks in it.'"

The vivid imagery in those three sentences took Hillary's speech to another level. By connecting with people on a visceral (not just intellectual) level, her words will be etched in their hearts and heads, and in the annals of time.

Having a name or slogan that conjures up a related image is increasingly important in our e-commerce society. In the old days of brick-and-mortar stores, we could walk by a business called Gap and see stylishly dressed mannequins in the window and instantly know the store sold clothes. We could even tell what *type* of clothes and decide if they fit our size and lifestyle. We could wander by a Harry & David and see the colorfully wrapped specialty foods (and even get free samples of their delicious chocolate-covered blueberries) and be drawn in by their mouth-watering displays.

On the World Wide Web, if there is a listing of stores that includes Gap and Harry & David, we wouldn't know what they sold unless we went to their website or were already familiar with them. If people read our business name online and it doesn't indicate what we do, people won't have a clue.

PAINT WORD PICTURES

Words are small shapes in the gorgeous chaos of the world.
They bring the world into focus, they corral ideas, they
hone thoughts, they paint watercolors of perception.
DIANE ACKERMAN

If people saw your business or product name online, would it mean anything to them? Could you give your company or offering a "word picture name" that conjures up a supporting image in your customers' mind's eye? Could you Aflac your idea so people see what you're saying?

A company wanted to introduce a new glue to the market and

wondered how they could compete with the number-one brand, Super Glue. I don't know the creative team that worked with this organization, but I'm guessing they asked themselves, What are the attributes of our glue? Well, for one thing, it's really strong. What do people think of when they imagine something really strong? An eight-hundred-pound gorilla!

That gave them a visual, meaningful, and memorable name: *Gorilla Glue.* Their newspaper ads feature a drawing of a lovable, yet powerful gorilla (we don't want our visual image to frighten people or scare customers away). Their ads POP! off the page and stick in the mind because they are visually arresting. More importantly, the name and image of Gorilla Glue seems to be POP!ing into people's minds when they're in stores because their product has been selling well.

Names and slogans that evoke images facilitate that all-important name recognition that means our brand is imprinted on people's minds and memories.

A techie told me he felt this "Make 'em see what you're saying" approach was one reason Ask Jeeves was initially successful in the beginning days of the web craze. Instead of calling their search engine service *SES* or something equally obtuse, the visionary creators humanized their computerized software program by giving it a human name and a visual image of a smiling butler at your service. They actually retired Jeeves in 2007 and renamed their search engine Ask.com. Why? Well, how many of you have a butler? How many of you know someone named Jeeves?

Brand names and slogans can become outdated or obsolete. Ask yourself, Will the visual icon I'm selecting for my product or business resonate with my audience over time? Is the slogan that used to work for us no longer current? Is what we're likening ourselves to not relevant to our target audience? If people smile and say, "I get it" or "I see now" when they hear or read about your offering, good for you. If they frown or appear puzzled, it's back to the drawing board, literally and figuratively.

CREATE YOUR OWN POP! ART

*There are three forms of visual art: Painting is art to
look at, sculpture is art you can walk around,
and architecture is art you can walk through.*

DAN RICE

I think there is a fourth type of visual art. POP! Art is communication you see and sound out in your mind. It is communication that creates mental images and pleasant sounds that engage our emotions and senses.

Want an example of a POP! Art name that conjures up a mental image every time you say it?

A group of talented entertainers had a unique interactive show that audiences loved. The problem was, how to break out? Every entertainer, speaker, director, conductor, and athletic event manager faces this challenge. There are dozens of plays, musicals, concerts, movies, and sports events competing for people's recreation and entertainment dollars. They realized they needed an ingenious gimmick to convince the paying public to plunk down sixty-five bucks to see their show rather than someone else's.

Hmm . . . how could they make their show stand out? There were other shows with music, juggling, magic, and audience participation. But none of the actors performed while painted *blue*. They could have called themselves the Funky Comedy Drumming Magic Act, but who could remember that? Why not call themselves what they *were*—the Blue Man Group. That is a simple but brilliant name because every time people read a review, poster, or ad, hear someone talk about the group, or remember what a great time they had at the show, it conjures up and reinforces their name.

That's POP! Art. It also was an inspired gimmick. Some people have a negative knee-jerk reaction to the word "gimmick," but it's defined in *Webster's New Universal Unabridged Dictionary* (which is where I got all the definitions in this book) as "an ingenious or novel device, scheme, or strategy designed to attract attention or increase appeal." Please reread that definition. Isn't that our goal? To attract attention and increase the appeal of our ideas, inventions, causes, or campaigns? What is a visual gimmick that could conjure up and reinforce your business or brand name every time people hear it, read it, or say it?

MAKE YOUR VERBIAGE VISUAL

Try to open a path through that maze,
put a little order in that chaos.
ISABEL ALLENDE

Do you have a process or methodology that is a maze? Is it so complicated or hard to explain, people look at you and say, "Huh?"

If you want to turn that confusing "Huh?" into an "I get it," turn your methodology into a visual sound bite. Take the first letter of each step in your process and turn it into an acronym that Cliff Notes your concept into something people can say and see. To work best, make sure your acronym spells something recognizable and meaningful so your audience will relate to it and want it.

For example, a lot of people feel they're not very good at remembering names. There are whole books on how to get better at doing this, but it's more likely that people will remember your process if you condense it into an easy-to-remember-and-apply three-letter acronym and affirmation . . . "I **C.A.N.** remember names."

C=Commit. I am going to get good at this, because I believe remembering and using someone's name is one of the best things I can do to let that person know she or he matters to me.

A = Attention on the face. Instead of being distracted or preoccupied, I will look into their eyes for at least three seconds so we make contact and both feel a connection.

N = Numerous repetitions. I will say their name out loud as soon as they say it, to be sure I heard it correctly (Betty vs. Betsy). Every time I glance at them, I will silently repeat their name to imprint it so, in the future, just looking at them triggers their name in my memory.

Another example of how it can help to place your concept in a short, easy-to-remember acronym was demonstrated by a campaign urging people to place emergency contact numbers on their cell phone. Following the London terrorist bombings in July 2005, rescue personnel discovered that many of the injured carried no information about next of kin. What this meant was not only did medical personnel not know the patient's medical history or possible allergies, making it difficult or dangerous to treat them, they didn't know who to contact who could supply them with that potentially life-saving information.

Bob Brotchie, a Cambridge-based paramedic who was familiar with the problems caused by this lack of information, originated the idea of suggesting cell phone owners simply add an entry to their cellular address directory with the names and phone numbers of family members to call in a crisis. I'm convinced that one of the reasons Bob's suggestion caught on internationally is because he made this process memorable and doable by Cliff Noting this admirable cause into the' three-letter acronym ICE, which stands for "In Case of Emergency." (By the way, if you haven't already done this, why not pull out your cell phone and do this now? It only takes seconds and it could save a life: yours.)

WHAT DOES YOUR OFFERING LOOK LIKE?

*When I examine myself and my methods of thought, I come to
the conclusion that the gift of fantasy has meant more to
me than my talent for absorbing positive knowledge.
Imagination is more important than intelligence.*

ALBERT EINSTEIN

Four enterprising British college students observed two converging trends: More and more people were keeping chickens as urban pets and the price of eggs was increasing. They put their heads together and designed a portable plastic chicken coop that could be placed in people's backyards so they could "have their eggs and cook 'em too."

What did they call their creation? Let's see, what does it look like? Well, the rounded exterior makes it look like an igloo. Look through the list of Core Words to see if anything POP!s. Chickens, hens, roosters, eggs. Hmm . . . that might work. Egg. Igloo. Combine them and you have *Eglu.* A clever name that has the media calling and customers flocking (sorry) to www.omlet.co.uk. By the way, this particular invention seems to spark people's imagination. Whenever I share this example in my programs, people in the audience often suggest alternative titles and slogans, such as, "The cluck stops here" and "Would you like all your eggs in one basket?" Eggsactly my point. Once you start thinking with this mindset, options POP! up everywhere.

A fellow professional speaker used much the same thinking to solve a problem she was experiencing with her pet. We had a particularly miserable winter and Nan Seimer's dog refused to "go" in the snow. Out of desperation, she designed a makeshift tent so her pooch could do his business, no matter how bad the weather. What to call her contraption? She drew it out on paper and showed it to others so they could group brainstorm. Well, it looked like a tent. A pup tent. No, that would get it confused with the old-fashioned pup tents used by the military. What does her pup do in the tent? There it is. *Poop Tent.* Don't laugh. Nan won an innovation award at a national conference with her creation and it's selling briskly at www.pooptent.com.

YOU CAN COMPARE APPLES TO ORANGES

The capacity to be puzzled is the premise of all creation,
be it in art or in science.
ERICH FROMM

The cover of the brilliant book *Freakonomics* proves that a picture can indeed be worth a thousand words. This book by Steven D. Levitt and Stephen J. Dubner won the 2005 Quill Book Award for Business, and I'm nominating it for the POP! Hall of Fame because it is a shining example of what happens when you take the time to create a Purposeful, Original, and Pithy message.

1. The pithy one-word title is a compelling example of how you can Alphabetize a Core Word (economics) to coin a new term and a one-of-a-kind brand name that belongs only to you.
2. The subtitle "A Rogue Economist Explains the Hidden Side of Everything" is purposeful in that it promises to reveal secrets that favorably positions it with its target audience of seasoned executives and business-book buyers who have "seen it all."
3. Their ads feature a marvelous Valley Girl endorsement from the *Wall Street Journal* that says, "If Indiana Jones were an economist, he'd be Steven D. Levitt." That comparison

linking the professor/author to the swashbuckling archae-
ologist/leading man broadens the topic's appeal, turning it
into a crossover book that's attracted mainstream readers
who might not normally be interested in this subject.

4. The authors pose such fascinating "POP! the Question" inquiries as "How is a beauty pageant like a crack dealer?"
and "What do school teachers and sumo wrestlers have in
common?" Aren't you intrigued? Phrasing these unexpected comparisons into questions engages our curiosity.
(This technique is covered in Chapter 13.)

5. The book cover Aflacs its premise that "Things are often
different than they appear," by showing a crisp green apple
with a slice cut out, revealing a juicy . . . *orange*. This made
their abstract concept concrete. This startling image has
become an identifiable visual brand that is now associated
with their work.

6. Furthermore, this visual contradiction is an excellent example of ContraBrand (covered in Chapter 10) in which
they challenge a common assumption; in this case the belief that you can't compare apples and oranges. They just
did! Kudos.

HOW TO USE THE AFLAC TECHNIQUE

*If a picture is worth a thousand words, please paint
me the Gettysburg Address.*
LEO ROSTEN

As with all things, there are exceptions to this rule. There are times
words are so eloquent they stand the test of time and are sufficient
in themselves. The question to ask yourself is, Are my words so eloquent they will stand the test of time? Will people remember my

message, my concept, the name or slogan of my business? If not, it's in your best interest to engage your audience's eyes and ears with the following steps.

Step 1. Ask yourself, Does my company or product name relate to something in the real world? Does it produce a *picture* or an appealing image in my customers' mind? Does it *sound* like something people are familiar with and fond of? If so, what?

Step 2. Ask, Is the name of my business or service nonsensical or significant only to me? Could I turn it into a meaningful acronym that's easier to say, remember, relate to, and use? What could that be? What are the Core Words, action steps, or primary principles I want to get across? How can I put those in their proper order so they spell out something that reminds people of the action they're supposed to take?

Step 3. Ask, How can I compare my abstract or complex concept to something concrete that exists in the real world? How can I link something intangible or coldly impersonal to something people can see, hear, feel, smell, touch, and like?

Step 4. Ask, What is an aspect of our service that solves a problem or addresses a need of our customers? Can that action or asset be built into a POP! Art name that causes people to see, imagine, and imprint our benefit to them?

9

Create the Next New Thing with the Half-and-Half Technique

*Creativity is like looking at the world through a kaleidoscope.
You look at a set of elements, the same ones everyone
else sees, but then reassemble those floating bits and
pieces into an enticing new possibility.*

ROSABETH MOSS KANTER

The popular FOX TV show *The O.C.* features a blended Christian and Jewish family. In December 2004, they ran an episode in which the family decided to combine their celebration of Christmas and Hanukkah. If you blend those words together, what do you get? *Chrismukkah.* That Half-and-Half word generated enormous free publicity in the media, word-of-mouth buzz, and top ratings.

In December 2005, the producers wisely capitalized on the visibility and record-number viewers generated by their previous *Chrismukkah* show by featuring a plot in which Seth planned a *Bar Mitzvahkah* for his "brother" Ryan. Their innovative term triggered even more watercooler conversations and turned it into a tell-a-friend phenomenon.

People are yearning to hear or see something they haven't encountered before. That's why the "next new thing" captures our attention. We have a Eureka Moment when we're introduced to something fresh. A quick way to entice people is to combine two aspects of your offering into a coined word that didn't exist before you crafted it.

For example, if you're a "foodie," you are probably aware of a style of cooking called fusion that combines two or more different ethnic cuisines. A restaurant chain capitalized on this concept by giving its Italian-Chinese restaurant a fused Half-and-Half name. Can you think of it? *Ciao Mein.*

A fast-food restaurant that specializes in hot dogs and beer came up with a fantastic Half-and-Half name. What are some synonyms for hot dog? Start a two-column list on a blank sheet of paper and place *frank, weiner,* and so forth on the left. What are some synonyms for beer? How about placing *brew, suds,* and *draft* in the right column? Okay, let's look for any links or for possible combinations that make sense. Hmm. Nada. Let's keep trying. What is beer served in? Well, *pitchers, glasses, bottles,* and *steins.* That's it. *Frank 'n Stein.*

COMPARE THE OPPOSITE ASPECTS
OF YOUR OFFERING

When opposites supplement each other, everything is harmonious.
Lao Tzu

Imagine you're a music producer who wants to promote a new type of dance music for teens. All you have to do is create a list of Core Words that describe old-fashioned music and current music. Get a piece of paper and draw a vertical line down the center to create two columns. Put the new terminology on the left and the old terminology on the right.

New-Style Music	Old-Style Music
Rap	Ballroom
Trance	Swing
Reggae	Twist
Stepping	Mashed Potato
Hip-hop	Bebop
Rave	Big Band

Start combining the words on the left with the words on the right. Or, blend the first half of a word on the left with the last half of a word on the right. Let's see. There's rap-room. Stepping in the mashed potatoes. There's a possibility. *Hip-bop*. It's half hip-hop and half bebop. In fact, I recently saw an article about the Country Music Awards Show. Guess what a reporter called a catchy tune that made you want to kick up your heels and hit the dance floor? *Hick Hop*.

COMBINE THE BEST AND THE WORST

> *It was the best of times, it was the worst of times,*
> *it was the age of wisdom, it was the age of foolishness,*
> *it was the epoch of belief, it was the epoch of incredulity,*
> *it was the season of Light, it was the season of Darkness,*
> *it was the spring of hope, it was the winter of despair . . .*
>
> INTRODUCTION TO CHARLES DICKENS'S
> *A TALE OF TWO CITIES*

Take a clue from Dickens's classic opening lines by combining the diametrically opposed qualities of your project. What is its bright side, its dark side? Its pros and cons? Also, compare aspects of your idea or item that aren't necessarily "right" or "wrong"; they're just different. Put the negative characteristics on the left and the positive characteristics on the right and then start creating combined words to see what POP!s.

For example, pediatric endocrinologist Francine Kaufman coined a classic Half-and-Half term for a health issue facing many Americans. She said, "A decade ago, if I saw a child with type 2 diabetes in my office, it would be such a rarity that case could be written up in a medical journal. Now, such children fill my clinic at Children's Hospital in Los Angeles." Many studies had linked obesity and diabetes, yet no one had the vision to link them in language. That is, until Dr. Kaufman did. She took half of *diabetes* and half of *obesity* and titled this phenomenon (and her book on this topic) *Diabesity*.

A fairly common occurrence these days is for twentysomethings to move back home to live with their parents. There are a lot of reasons for this, including that many of them are paying off student loans and it's hard to find a job that allows them to be self-supporting. Plus, as one of my son's friends says, "You can only eat so much Ramen. It's nice to have Mom's homemade cooking again."

I've seen numerous articles on this subject and a variety of self-proclaimed experts discussing it on TV. One particularly smart individual cornered the market on this topic. How? Ian Pierpoint, a senior vice president with Synovate, coined a Half-and-Half term that's established him as the media's go-to resource on this phenomenon of young people who are half adults and half adolescents. He calls them *Adultescents*.

Half-and-Half words are almost guaranteed to stand out in the crowd—because there *is* no crowd. When you coin a term, you go to the head of the class. You are the one who will get called by the networks to be the guest expert on this concept you've created. You are the one who will get quoted in newspapers, profiled in magazines, discussed in chat rooms, and e-mailed about as your new term takes on a life of its own.

CAPTURE WORDPLAYS THAT CROSS YOUR MIND

"While we were talking, a thought crossed my mind."
"Short trip."
CHARACTERS CONVERSING IN JOSEPH R. GARBER'S
NOVEL *WHIRLWIND*

Comedian Rich Hall invented a term for words that aren't in the dictionary but should be. He calls them *sniglets*. During his stint on HBO's *Not Necessarily the News* in the 1980s, he hosted a regular segment featuring humorous words he and other people had made up to describe things that had no official definition. The *Washington Post* runs an annual contest selecting the best of the best. Standouts include:

- staremaster (workout buffs who constantly look at themselves in the mirror)
- giraffiti (vandalism sprayed very, very high)
- inoculatte (coffee lovers who mainline their favorite beverage)
- intaxacation (euphoria at getting a tax refund, which lasts until you realize it was your money to begin with)
- reintarnation (coming back to life as a hillbilly)
- gramstand (to brag excessively about one's grandchildren)
- déjà view (when there's nothing but reruns on TV)
- Internut (someone who's constantly on the web)

When you come up with your own sniglets, be sure to write them down on the back of your W9 Form. Review these gems when you're preparing a presentation or planning to write an article to see if any might spice up your content.

MAKE UP YOUR OWN MALAPOPISMS

Has this rookie exceeded your expectations?
REPORTER

I'd say he's done more than that.
YOGI BERRA

If you make a malapropism (defined by Webster's as "an act or habit of misusing words, especially by the confusion of words that sound the same"), don't immediately correct it. Stop for a moment to see if there's potential in your error. With luck, you could turn it into a . . . wait for it . . . MalaPOPism.

For example, the other day I was trying to say *perpetuity* but *pubertuity* came out. That slip of the tongue produced a newly minted Half-and-Half word that could turn into a career for a psychologist who could write and present a paper on this topic for her annual industry association conference and become a media resource sharing her insights on TV and radio about adults who behave like teenagers who don't want to grow up.

Kids come up with these unintentional new words all the time. Years ago, I was explaining the concept of serendipity to my son Andrew. He came up to me later in the day and said, "You know, Mom, I really like that concept of *serendestiny*." That is a sublime Half-and-Half word that could be turned into a book or presentation about how people can be alert to and act upon those chance encounters some people call coincidences.

I drove by an old-fashioned theater a few days before Halloween and laughed out loud at the movie marquee. They were showing the popular audience-participation film *Rocky Horror Picture Show* every night that week. In case you're not familiar with this fan favorite, people dress up as their favorite character, sing along with the tunes, and actually get up in front of the screen and act out their favorite scenes. What caught my attention was the clever label they had given this half movie–half karaoke event: *Movie-oke*.

A music appreciation professor at my son's college was a natural master of this technique. Tom understood after the first few classes why Dr. Cole was so popular. He assigned movies such as *The Red Violin* and *Amadeus* as homework. He would play a meolody on the piano and then share behind-the-scenes tidbits about the composer. He even (gasp) introduced students to opera, although he wasn't content to call it something ordinary. He coined a Half-and-Half title for his lecture on this topic: *Opera-tunity*.

HOW TO USE THE HALF-AND-HALF TECHNIQUE

I was forced to go to a positive-thinking seminar. I couldn't stand it. So I went outside to the parking lot and let half the air out of everybody's tires. As they came out I said, "So . . . are your tires half full or half empty?"

ADAM CHRISTING

Ready to coin your own Half-and-Half term that Cliff Notes the multifaceted essence of your concept into a tight sound bite?

Step 1. Take out a piece of paper and draw a vertical line down the center. Put half your Core Words in the left column and the other half in the right column.

Step 2. Now, take the first half of each word in the left column and blend it with the last half of the words in the right column. Write down any possibilities that POP!

Step 3. Then, take the first half of the words in the right column and blend them with the last half of the words in the left column. Continue until you've gone through your list and tried all the different variations. Keep your eyes and ears open for a blended word that captures the dual nature of your issue in one never-before-seen term. In short, a way for your idea or invention to get noticed and remembered.

Step 4. Linus Pauling said, "The best way to have a good idea is to have lots of ideas." Be sure to put your thoughts on paper so you can *see* all the different options. Your mind will leap to conclusions (in a good way) because it will visually mix and match the different phrases. The more options you generate, the more likely you are to crystallize the perfect title or tagline.

Step 5. Remember this is not just wordplay, it is word *profit*. While speaking at a Meeting Planners International conference, I met a sales manager for Seattle's Convention Visitors Bureau. She told me that Seattle had hit the jackpot by coining an original brand that's generated a billion dollars (yes, that's a *b*) in free publicity. Their attention-grabbing Half-and-Half term—*Metro-Natural*—cleverly captures the dual nature of the city's cosmopolitan yet parklike setting. Well done.

Ready to learn another way to help your offering break out? On to the next chapter where we suggest you introduce something that causes people to rethink what they believe to be true.

10

Turn Assumptions Upside Down with ContraBrand

The opposite of a correct statement is a false statement. But the opposite of a profound truth may well be another profound truth.

NIELS BOHR

I was walking through the Chicago airport when a magazine at a newsstand caught my eye and literally stopped me in my tracks. I was so shocked I actually backtracked to check it out. Why? The cover headline on this particular issue of *Newsweek* screamed in huge capital letters, "TV IS GOOD FOR YOUR KIDS." Only when I looked closer did I see the caveat, in much smaller type in the lower right-hand corner: "No, it's not."

What's the point? When was the last time you walked out of your way to pick up a copy of a weekly magazine?

There are probably dozens of offerings similar to yours in the marketplace. How can you differentiate yourself so people have a compelling reason to pick you rather than your competitors?

One of the best ways is to figure out how we can make what we're saying or selling counterintuitive. There were dozens of magazines, all sitting face out, on that shelf, but the one featuring the controversial claim was the only one that caught my attention.

STATE THE OPPOSITE, NOT THE OBVIOUS

"The cat sat on the mat" is not the beginning of a story.
"The cat sat on the dog's mat" is.

JOHN LECARRÉ

John LeCarré's insightful observation holds true for all communication. If we state the obvious, our words just sit there and leave people apathetic. We want to intrigue people so they, as radio host Paul Harvey would say, are eager to know "the rest of the story."

How can you make your title, tagline, or marketing message contradictory so people are compelled to know more?

Take Valentine's Day. Please. As reported by Oliver Barker in the February 13, 2006, issue of *USA Today*, Valentine's Day is the third-biggest gift-giving holiday (after Christmas and Mother's Day). Smart entrepreneurs and organizations are keeping that in mind and targeting the vast untapped market of singles who may be spending the day alone.

For example, there's a snarky e-card with the punch line "Valentine bites" available at the American Greetings website. Those going solo can buy bittersweet "commiseration candies" imprinted with "I don't care" at www.despair.com. Many Hallmark card stores sold out of their "Love Is a Bear" teddy bears, which wore a T-shirt inscribed, "My girlfriends are more fun."

Another holiday novelty that got lots of free press (always a good thing) is the Christmas tree that turned a holiday tradition on its head. Literally. Picture the normal triangular tree, wide at the bottom and narrowing to the star on top. Now, turn it upside down and you get the inverted Christmas tree that Hammacher Schlemmer couldn't keep in stock . . . at $599.95 a POP! Target had three upside-down trees on its website, which touted their best attribute: "Leaves more room on the floor for gifts!"

What's the point? Holidays offer lots of opportunities to "swim against the tide." Family gatherings are often optimistically depicted as being Walton-like when, for many people, they're more often like TV's dysfunctional Simpsons. How can you make the most of this disparity? Simply ask yourself, What is the elephant-in-the-room aspect of this time of year? How can I write an article about what is *really* going on? How can I invent a product that addresses the *underbelly* of my issue? How can my business create a service that resolves or relieves a "secret pain" that is felt by many but rarely admitted?

WHAT ARE YOU SAYING THAT FLIES IN THE FACE OF CURRENT WISDOM?

To believe is very dull. To doubt is intensely engrossing.
OSCAR WILDE

Journalist Steven Johnson wrote a book called *Everything Bad Is Good for You* in which he claims, among other things, that video games are actually healthy for teens because they provide a cognitive workout that increases motor control. His "Say what?!" assertion earned him a lengthy profile in the *Washington Post* in which he freely admitted, "If this makes people mad, it's achieved its goal. I could have written a more balanced book, but that is the kind of book nobody listens to."

I am not suggesting we compromise our integrity and create sensationalistic slogans simply to get attention. I *am* suggesting that challenging a norm can serve people (and us) if a bold claim stops people in their mental tracks and motivates them to rethink outdated assumptions. Saying and doing the same thing as everyone else is guaranteed to keep you one of many. Is there a legitimate way you can rile emotion and create a debate so people are motivated to check you out?

Sometimes, the biggest advances are made when someone dares to say, "You're operating with incorrect convictions. Your emperor has no clothes." Saying something routine doesn't have the ability to shake people out of their routine. Sometimes we have to hit a nerve in order for people to give our message a chance.

An interesting example of this principle is a book that was featured in every major magazine and on every national TV talk show in the United States and was one of the bestselling books of 2004. First, the backstory.

Greg Behrendt, a former script consultant to the HBO sitcom *Sex and the City*, was kibitzing with the female writers for the show. Instead of brainstorming the next episode, one of the women was complaining about the supposedly perfect date she'd been on a few weeks before. She described how the two of them had really hit it off and they'd had a magical evening. The guy asked for her phone number and promised to call, then never did. Her female friends were quick to sympathize, reassuring her she was a great catch, the guy must have "commitment issues," and that he was probably really busy.

After listening to their well-intended but naive advice, Behrendt, the sole man in the room, couldn't stand it anymore and interrupted with this stop-tiptoeing-around-the-truth observation: "Or maybe he's just not that into you."

Gasp. His claim that the guy would have followed up if he had really been interested contradicted the friends' supportive spin about "getting dumped" and became the title of his (and Liz Tuccillo's) bestseller, *He's Just Not That Into You: The No-Excuses Truth to Understanding Guys*.

Imagine if they had called their book *Strategies for Successful Dating*. Boring. One reason this book generated so much buzz and became so POP!ular is because its gloves-off title promised it would be a tell-it-like-it-is read.

THE QUESTION ISN'T WHETHER IT'S TRUE, BUT IS IT NEW?

Someone's boring me. I think it's me.

DYLAN THOMAS

I meet many people who naively believe that if their subject is important, it will find an audience. Not so. Just because you're passionate about a topic doesn't mean other people will be too. Important isn't enough; it's got to be innovative. Why would they plunk down their money to buy your book, attend your workshop, or hire your services if they already know or agree with what you're saying?

What startles people, stops them in their mental tracks, and gets a rise out of them is to dispute what they believe is right. Now we have a disagreement. Now they're engaged. Ask yourself, What is a norm, a common belief, in my industry? How can my idea or invention be the antithesis of that? If your competitors' products are small, maybe yours can be large. If they're slow, be fast. If they're cheap, be high-end. What does everyone assume to be true? Pick a title, tagline, or headline that disputes that and makes people blink in surprise and say, "What?!"

Professional speaker Mary Jane Mapes works with organizations that want to improve their communication. She was hired by an association to deal with a particularly irascible board member who was holding up progress and making everyone miserable. Her contact told her, "We've tried everything to work with this guy and nothing's worked. Oh well," she sighed resignedly, "you know the old saying, 'You can't teach a pig to sing. It just wastes your time and annoys the pig.'"

Aha! Mary Jane has an impressive track record of being able to resolve just about any conflict. All she had to do was turn that phrase around to create a perfect ContraBrand title, *You CAN Teach Pigs to Sing*.

Ask yourself, Is there a secret in my subject? Is there a delicate subject my clients are tiptoeing around? Is there some embarrassing aspect about my message that people won't admit? If so, be the bold one to break it out in the open. The fact that you are daring to surface a contentious, sensitive, or feared issue can grab people's attention even in the midst of their rush-rush life.

A client (name withheld) is working on a book called *The Cancer Conspiracy*. Her bold assertion, backed with evidence, is that "the war on cancer is not being won—it's not even being fought. Why? There's no money in curing cancer—there's money in treating cancer." Her troubling allegation is based on what she's witnessed within the pharmaceutical industry as an employee for one of the large drug companies. That is certainly a sweeping claim, yet she feels strongly that people deserve to be made aware of the disturbing cover-ups taking place. She's the first to admit there are exceptions to her deliberately overstated premise, but she's clear that if that title serves in attracting public interest and media attention for this vital issue, it's worth it.

HOW TO USE THE CONTRABRAND TECHNIQUE

Only dead fish swim with the stream all the time.
LINDA ELLERBEE

Is your message thought-provoking? Does it prompt people to reassess the way they've always done things? Are you introducing stop-'em-in-their-tracks epiphanies that cause people to question their automatic behavior? Is your product the exact opposite of everything else on the shelf? If so, well done. If not, use this technique to make your message more audacious and your offering more unusual so it stands out from the crowd instead of getting lost in the crowd.

Step 1. *What am I saying that is counterintuitive?* Please write down all the norms that are accepted about your topic, industry, or profession. What do people believe to be true? Now, ask yourself, How can I say the opposite of that? How can I introduce something that causes people to rethink their assumptions and question their current beliefs?

Step 2. *Where am I suggesting that people challenge authority instead of giving blind allegiance? How can I point out how the real world works so people aren't continuing to operate with self-sabotaging naiveté?* Cynthia Shapiro worked as a human resources director for many years. She witnessed disturbing behavior in her industry and decided she could no longer stay silent about what she felt was a travesty of justice. Her book, *Corporate Confidential: 50 Secrets Your Company Doesn't Want You to Know—and What to Do About Them*, was published by St. Martin's Press. Her book has created a lot of debate because it dared to claim HR departments aren't acting in *your* best interests. They're acting in the *company's* best interests. Cynthia knew from experience that many employees naively believed that personal revelations made to their HR rep were private and wouldn't be used against them. Wrong. She shared examples of how trusting individuals who confessed to personal problems or health challenges unknowingly compromised their promotability.

Step 3. *Where am I daring to be politically incorrect? How am I being a whistle-blower? How am I blowing the lid off a secret that I believe deserves to be revealed?* Michael Moore's films *Roger and Me* and *Fahrenheit 9/11* introduced and explored underbelly issues that created heated debate, which built buzz for his films. Many people went to see them simply because they had to find out for themselves what all the fuss was about.

Step 4. *How is my product addressing a problem no one wants to talk about but everyone desperately needs to discuss? How is my product revolutionary in that it does something people thought couldn't be done? In what way is my invention the polar opposite of what people expect?*

In our next chapter, we'll offer more ways to bring a unique perspective to an issue or invention that makes it distinctively yours.

11

Make the Familiar Fresh with Meaningful Metaphors

I never met-a-phor I didn't like.
RICHARD LEDERER

Jan Holman wanted to start her own business, speaking, writing, and consulting about the topic of managing money and growing wealth. That posed a challenge because there are hundreds of experts on that subject. Even though she had impressive credentials as the spokesperson for a nationally known financial firm, it would be hard to break out of the pack because she had so much competition.

I simply asked, "What do you do when you're not working?" She replied, "I play golf." I said, "We're in business."

We got out a piece of paper and drew a line down the center of the page. We put her topic, *Managing Money*, on the top of the left column and her hobby, *Golf*, on the top of the right column. We then started brainstorming and writing down every golf-associated term we could think of: *fairway, clubs, woods, irons, tee, driver, green,* and so on in the right-hand column.

Next, we listed the phrases related to making smart investments on the left, including such Core Words as *savings, debt, interest, cash, credit cards,* and *money*.

Then we compared the two columns looking for correlations and connections. Hmm. *Money. Green.* That's a catchy connection. How about *Go for the Green?*

That title is short and it works for both sides of the equation because the term is used in golf and in finance. She now had a meaningful and singular metaphorical approach to her topic that is based on her life experience and expertise.

We didn't stop there. We kept exploring the metaphor, looking for other similarities between golf and investing. Guess how many chapters her book ought to have? That's right, eighteen. Her summary could be called The 19th Hole. And instead of calling these *strategies*, let's use another golf-related word and call these *links*. Hmm . . . how about "18 Links Between High-Performance Golf and High-Yield Investing?"

Now that's a POP! title and subtitle. It's purposeful because Jan's target audience is executives who have the authority to buy books for their staff and who have the budget to hire her to deliver convention and corporate presentations. Many CEOs play golf and are interested in growing their portfolio, so this metaphor positioned her with her intended customers. Furthermore, there weren't any other financial advisors using this metaphor so she had succeeded in crafting a one-of-a-kind approach in a crowded field.

HOW ARE YOU EXPRESSING YOUR INDIVIDUALITY?

Individuality of expression is the beginning and the end of all art.
JOHANN WOLFGANG VON GOETHE

Metaphors, defined by Webster's as "a figure of speech in which a word or phrase literally denoting one kind of object or idea is used in place of another to suggest a likeness between them," are a great way to create a message that reflects what's special about you while giving you a unique approach to a common subject.

A program participant said, "I agree with this, I just don't know how to find a metaphor." You can find an analogy that gives you a fresh take on a familiar topic by tapping into the "Triple A's":

Avocation: What is a hobby or recreational activity you do for fun?

Achievement: What is an accomplishment you're proud of?

Adversity: What is a challenge you've overcome?

The beauty of drawing upon a Triple A analogy is that it is specific to you. By definition, it is not common or copied. You will be the first to use it because you created it. I will give three examples of how others developed personally significant metaphors by capitalizing on their Avocation, Achievement, and Adversity—and then show how you can become the sole authority on your topic by plumbing your past.

WHAT'S AN AVOCATION THAT BRINGS YOU JOY?

Eighty percent of life is showing up.
WOODY ALLEN

I think 80 percent of your message's success is showing up *first*. That's why metaphors can be so effective. Using a metaphorical approach to introduce your idea helps people see it fresh, as if for the first time.

An executive was challenged because several of his department heads were micromanaging their employees. These perfectionists frequently redid their team's work because it didn't meet their high standards. No matter how many times Kevin counseled them that their staff members would never learn how to do their jobs right if they kept rescuing them, they couldn't seem to resist coming in and correcting their errors.

Since what he was doing wasn't working, it was time to try another approach. I asked him what he did in his spare time. He said, "I'm a private pilot." I said, "Perfect. Tell me about the flight instructor who certified you."

He smiled and said, "My first one was awful. She was a Nervous Nellie who constantly pointed out what I was doing wrong. I never did anything right in her eyes. As a result, I started second-guessing all my decisions. I almost quit because I was so discouraged. She wasn't there one Saturday so another instructor took me up. He was the exact opposite. We were doing touch and go's [quick landings and take-offs] and I was bringing the plane in too hot [fast]. Instead of yelling at me, he simply asked, 'What's your airspeed?' As part of that lesson, I had to 'stall' the plane so I would know how to recover. Lights flash and alarms go off to warn you you're about to crash so it's a pretty chaotic scene. Instead of grabbing the stick, he just let me figure out how to stabilize the plane on my own. He's the reason I kept with it and finally got my pilot's license."

I asked Kevin, "Could you share that story at your next staff meeting so your managers can 'see' that they're doing what that first flight instructor did? It gives them a face-saving way to look at the consequences of criticizing and rescuing, and chances are they'll back off and let their employees 'fly the plane' themselves."

Kevin said, "It's worth a try." Later he got back to me to say that not only did they "get" the message, but also "Let them fly the plane" has become their verbal shorthand for "stop micromanaging."

WHAT'S AN ACHIEVEMENT YOU'RE PROUD OF?

*A good title should be like a good metaphor: it should intrigue
without being too baffling or too obvious.*
WALKER PERCY

Maryellen Lipinski was a nationally known keynoter on the subject
of change. Her unique take on the topic was based on her experience as a champion roller skater. She would roll up a ramp to the
stage on her skates and demonstrate different techniques, comparing them to the process of how organizations and individuals can
"Skate Through Change." She would talk about how we can make
progress while moving backward and would deliberately trip herself
up and then point out the importance of "falling down seven times,
geting up eight."

You can understand why she was such a popular speaker. One
problem. She'd been giving this speech for years and was ready to
practice what she preached and do something different. She was
nearing the big 5-0 and wanted to shake up her life. So, this California girl moved from Manhattan Beach to North Carolina and began searching for property so she could build her own home.

Maryellen found a dream lot with a spectacular view high in the
mountains. After several months of experiencing nothing but frustration with contractors who didn't show up on time (or at all), she
decided, "I've got a Ph.D. I can build a house." And that's what she
did. Several months later, Maryellen settled into a log home she had
helped build from scratch.

The master of the metaphor, she began developing a new
keynote to reflect her new life. She realized that building a quality
house from the ground up is much like building a quality life from
the ground up. She listed the similarities between the two topics
(for example, establishing a firm foundation and making sure you're

wired for success) and named her new book and presentation *Life Under Construction*. Way to go, Maryellen.

WHAT ADVERSITY HAVE YOU FACED?

Instead of seeking new landscapes, develop new eyes.
MARCEL PROUST

Patricia Nordrup is a dynamic woman in her late seventies who is the picture of determination. She has overcome incredible odds and has lived to tell the story. Literally.

When she was in her thirties, she awoke in the middle of the night with a terrible headache. She actually remembers something bursting in her head. She took some aspirin and told her husband, and they went to the doctor first thing the next morning. Her physician gave her a pelvic exam (?!) and reassured her it had probably been a bad migraine. Over the next few weeks, Pat found it increasingly difficult to think straight. After repeated visits to a variety of doctors who all dismissed her belief that she had suffered a stroke (after all, she was relatively young and the picture of health), she was finally correctly diagnosed.

Pat's husband was an inventor who counted on Pat to type his notes and research papers. With her fingers partially frozen and her mind uncooperative, Pat had to reteach herself how to write, problem solve, and communicate. Tired of being treated as if she were dumb, she created a system to concentrate despite her challenges. She went to college and trained to become a school counselor so she could teach students with learning disabilities to stay focused, using the techniques she had developed herself. This amazing woman has written a book about her experiences. You might be able to guess her metaphor title: *Stroke of Genius*.

An axiom in the professional speaking world is to "dance with who or what brung ya." In other words, instead of spouting the same old, same old rhetoric, what is a pivotal event, extraordinary experience, or inspiring challenge from your past? The more unusual your signature story, the more unique your message.

HOW TO USE THE MEANINGFUL METAPHOR TECHNIQUE

See everything as if for the first or last time. Then your days on Earth will be filled with glory.
BETTY SMITH

Are you ready to access your Triple A analogies to create an evocative metaphor for your process or priority project? The goal is to come up with an innovative approach that helps people see your idea or offering as if for the first time so they take notice instead of walk on by.

Step 1. Draw three vertical lines on a blank piece of paper to divide it into four columns of equal size.

Step 2. At the top of the left most column, write in your topic or the priority project you're brainstorming, whether it's an issue you're trying to bring to the attention of the public or a new gadget you've created. List all your Core Words in that column.

Step 3. In the next column over, write in the word *Avocation* at the top. Then, list the activities you like to do in your spare time. What is a hobby or recreational activity that takes up most of your weekends? A special interest you love doing just for the fun of it? Do you sail? Sing in a choir? Garden? Ride horses? Coach your daughter's soccer team? Write down the terminology associated with this pastime.

Step 4. Write in the word *Achievement* at the top of the next column. What is an accomplishment that you're particularly proud of? Did you go back to school and earn your college degree while working full-time? Travel to a foreign country solo? Build your own house from the ground up, like Maryellen? Mentally reenact what was involved in completing that goal. Write down the Core Words you use when describing that process.

Step 5. In the final column on the right, write the word *Adversity* at the top. What is an obstacle you've overcome? Were you unfairly fired? Have you rebounded from a difficult divorce? Survived a hurricane that devastated your community? Relive that experience and write the key words that crop up when explaining it.

Step 6. Next, look at what you've recorded in the Avocation, Achievement, and Adversity columns and ask, Which of these experiences are similar in some way to the essence of my topic or product? Where is there a comparison or commonality?

Step 7. You'll often find parallel phrases between your topic/project and one of your Triple A's. Study similarities between the two experiences and write down how _____ is like _____. Ask yourself, Instead of just talking about my subject or product, how can I start with an analogy so people get the point and see my subject and product from a different perspective? How can I share a personal example of a hobby, accomplishment, or conquered challenge and then compare it to my issue or invention so people see it as if for the first time?

12

Win Buy-In by Capitalizing on POP! Culture

Ideas are like rabbits. You get a couple and learn how to handle them, and pretty soon you have a dozen.

JOHN STEINBECK

Washington, DC, is famous for its monuments, government buildings, and Smithsonian museums. Tourists travel from around the world to visit its attractions, but they get tired of trekking from site to site during the hot summer. A clever business-man introduced Segways, the motorized scooters you stand on, as an alternative form of transportation and as a unique way to see the town. Not content to call his touring company something mun-dane, he capitalized on a POP! icon and called it *Segs in the City*.

One way to generate dozens of innovative ideas is to start listen-ing to what's discussed around the watercooler. Did you see the movie *The Sixth Sense*, in which the young boy says the classic line, "I see dead people"? I want you to see POP! icons. Keep your eyes and ears open for the buzz phrases that are on the tip of everyone's tongue. Verbally piggybacking on those iconic phrases is a way to hitch your idea's wagon to their star and take a ride on their preestablished fame.

Are you familiar with the phrase "Jump the shark," used to

describe someone who has gone over the top? It originated from the *Happy Days* TV show. After the show had been on the air for years, the writers were frantically looking for fresh story lines. Almost out of desperation, they produced an episode in which Fonzie and the gang went water-skiing and—you saw this coming, didn't you?—Fonzie jumped a shark. That phrase has become a catchphrase used when a show is running out of creative gas and starts stretching for plots.

Fast-forward to 2005. Tom Cruise has just appeared on *Oprah* to profess his passion for Katie Holmes. Not content to simply say he cares for her, Tom leaps onto the couch and starts jumping up and down while announcing to the world, "I'm in love!" The headline of the article? You got it. "Jump the Couch"—the new catchphrase for when someone goes off the deep end.

CORRELATE UNTIL IT CLICKS

All thought is a feat of association: having what's in front of you bring up something in your mind that you almost didn't know you knew. Putting this and that together. That click.

ROBERT FROST

A woman wanted to open a yoga studio and was trying to come up with the perfect name. She had been racking her brain for weeks and had nothing to show for it. We sat down with a pile of popular magazines and started flipping through them, looking for something that caught our eye.

A full-page ad featuring tennis champion Pete Sampras wearing a milk mustache and a T-shirt with the slogan "Got milk?" stopped us in our tracks. We looked at each other with big smiles and said simultaneously, "Got Yoga?" That is a short, fun name she could feature in huge letters on her business cards and storefront. It will help her business stand out in a directory with dozens of fitness centers and compel people to check her out.

Two twentysomething advertising guys, Jason Hoff and Jeff Candido, created what I predict will become one of the top ten slogans of this century. These two had been hired to design a memorable slogan for a tourism promotion campaign for Las Vegas. The two sat in a room and just kept "noodling and doodling" (aka brainstorming and sketching). They verbally Ping Ponged ideas back and forth about how they could get across the message that Las Vegas was changing its 1990s focus from being a family-friendly vacation destination to a new emphasis on being an R-rated resort for adults.

Finally, one of them casually mentioned a motto previously attributed to sailors and traveling salesmen: "What happens here, stays here." There it was, the iconic phrase "What happens in Vegas stays in Vegas" that has become the "Where's the beef?" of our time.

The Professional Bull Riders Association holds their annual finals in Las Vegas. This rough and tumble event features 160-pound cowboys trying to stay on top of 1,000-pound bucking bulls for eight seconds. Most of the riders are violently thrown off before the whistle blows. In a brilliant display of trading off their location's brand name, they created a fitting slogan for their 2005 Finals: "What happens here, hurts here."

MUSE IT OR LOSE IT

Writers get to live life twice.
Anne Lamott

The beauty of becoming a POP! practitioner is it's a way to live life twice. When you read, hear, see, or experience something out of the ordinary, mentally step back and ask, How can I use that? Where's the lesson learned? Is there a way to incorporate that into my communication or marketing message to make it more interesting?

If you do this, everyone and everything in your world becomes a source of material. Broadcaster Diane Sawyer has said, "I have found there is no substitute for paying attention." Agreed. Start paying attention to whatever captures your attention. If it stops you in your mental tracks, it will probably stop other people in their mental tracks too.

I will always remember walking with former National Geographic photographer Dewitt Jones along a Maui beach. We were talking about something when Dewitt suddenly stopped, whipped out a pencil, and scribbled something down. We went a few more paces, then he pulled out his notepad again and made another note. After doing this a couple more times, I finally asked, "Dewitt, what are you doing?"

He said, "If an idea pops into my head and I don't make a note of it, it's gone. I take a notepad with me everywhere I go. If something occurs to me, it doesn't matter where I am, I jot it down and then I know it's there waiting for me when I'm ready for it."

INK IT WHEN YOU THINK IT

It often happens that things come into the mind in a more finished
form than could have been achieved after much study.
FRANÇOIS DE LA ROCHEFOUCAULD

Dewitt is right. The muse has a mind and a schedule of her own. All it asks is that when it gives us an idea, we write it down. As long as we do, it'll keep coming around. If we don't appreciate the epiphanies that POP! into our heads and make a note of them, the muse gets offended and says, "Bye-bye, I've got better things to do."

When an idea comes to mind, you have been given a gift. Your mind has just noticed something extraordinary. Disparate thoughts have suddenly coalesced into an epiphany. Synapses have fired in a new way and produced an insight. Creative lightning has just struck. If we don't jot them down, they're gone, never to return. What clay is to a potter, occurrences are to POP! practitioners.

Turn your friends into POP! practitioners and ask them to be on the lookout for interesting items that relate to your offering. On www.SamHornPOP.wordpress.com, I ask people to send me innovative ads, one-of-a-kind business or product names, funny commercials, and stop-'em-in-their-tracks slogans that have caught their attention. One of my favorites came from a friend who told me that when the final Star Wars movie was being released in the summer of 2005, Lucas Films forged a merchandising agreement with one of the top-ten bestselling toys of all time. What was the POP! icon name they gave this Star Wars version of Mr. Potato Head? *Darth Tater.*

By the way, when I went to see *Revenge of the Sith* over the July 4 weekend, I got further evidence of Lucas Films' marketing brilliance. The box office featured a movie poster with a banner affixed to it that trumpeted, "May the Fourth Be with You!" Bravo.

PAY ATTENTION TO WHAT "MADE YA LOOK"

In the fields of observation, chance favors only the prepared mind.
Louis Pasteur

Some of the best POP! practitioners are cookbook authors and publishers. Cookbooks are perennial bestsellers because preparing and eating food is part of everyone's day. The problem is, it's a saturated market. Just walk into any bookstore and you'll see the shelves groaning with cookbooks on everything from how to make omelets to how to prepare meals in ten minutes or less.

Since every topic and title has been "taken," so to speak, publishers have been forced to get creative so their new releases won't get lost on those crowded shelves. They have been more than up to the challenge. Just a few of the clever titles that have helped these books succeed in a saturated market are *Great Eggspectations, A Grill's Best Friends, King of the Grill, Boy Meets Grill,* and *Let the Flames Begin.*

Who knows, the authors of that last book may have been brainstorming their title during the opening ceremonies of the Olympics. Maybe they heard the iconic announcement, "Let the Games begin," and bingo, there was their title.

You may be wondering what the rules are about using someone else's intellectual property. Well, that's a book in itself. If you have questions about whether it is appropriate to make a play on words with a specific POP! culture phrase, check with a trademark attorney to determine whether your proposed phrase is legal or would violate someone's registered trademark.

HOW TO USE THE POP! CULTURE TECHNIQUE

An abiding tenet of TV is that viewers don't want new shows,
they want new shows that remind them of old shows.
FRED ALLEN

Ready to create a topical title or tagline by riffing off a popular saying to help your product POP! off the shelf, your article POP! off the page, and for your idea to keep POP!ing into people's mind?

Step 1. Go to the magazine section of your local library or bookstore. Select several popular publications, such *People, Time, Newsweek, Reader's Digest,* and *Fast Company.*

Step 2. Review your W9 Form and your Core Words so they are freshly imprinted in your mind. Start thumbing through the magazines and newspapers, looking for related headlines, captions, slogans, or ad copy that POP! off the page.

Step 3. Write down any and all pertinent phrases that catch your attention. Now, let the wordplay begin. Substitute your product's name into the subject line. Insert your theme or topic into an iconic phrase to give it your personalized touch.

Step 4. Watch TV shows and movies with a new mindset. If something makes you chuckle or you hear a particularly pithy insight that causes you to reflect, write it down. Later on, review your notes and pick out any high-potential phrases that are somehow related to your idea, business, or service. Insert your Core Words and rearrange the phrases to create a title that helps your communication POP!

Step 5. Remember to muse it so you don't lose it. When a potential title or tagline comes to mind, ink it when you think it.

Our next chapter points out another technique that can help you engage your audience's interest and cause them to consider your offering.

13

POP! the Question to Engage Curiosity

A prudent question is one half of wisdom.
SIR FRANCIS BACON

Do you remember Regis Philbin's "Is that your final answer?" on the popular TV show *Who Wants to Be a Millionaire?* Those simple words were repeated around the world and achieved POP! icon status.

Imagine if Regis had simply said, "You need to make a decision now." Doesn't POP!, does it? Declarative statements sit on the page. Questions engage.

The best POP! messages are so enticing, people can't help but be intrigued. If your message simply explains what you have to offer, it's easy for people to keep their mental arms crossed. Straightforward explanations don't have the power to pull people out of a "prove you're worth my valuable time and money" mentality.

Could you instead phrase your slogan, title, or introduction as a question?

Declarative statements telling why our product or service is worth buying are one-way communication that can be perceived as mini-lectures. Questions set up two-way communication because they ask for feedback. Listeners, viewers, or readers are more likely to respond to interactive messages.

COULD YOU MAKE YOUR MESSAGE MYSTERIOUS?

The most beautiful thing we can experience is the mysterious.
It is the source of all true art and science.
ALBERT EINSTEIN

Look at your slogan or pitch. Is it composed purely of declarative statements? Are you leaving interest on the table because you're telling instead of asking? Could you add some mystery to your slogan by turning it into a question?

Think about the former CapitalOne ads that featured actor David Spade. Every ad ended with a voiceover, "What's in your wallet?" Didn't you almost automatically wonder, "Hmm, what *is* in my wallet?"

Do your title and tagline go in one ear and out the other? They might be more "sticky" if they are crafted into a question. Sticky questions capture people's attention initially and continue to POP! into their mind over time.

Please note I used the word *crafted*. Perfectly designed marketing messages are a byproduct of rewriting and fine-tuning. When done well, they cause customers to both hear what we said and to consider what we said. Instead of just passively observing our words, they're actively reflecting on how this relates to their life.

If you go to www.oprah.com, you'll see a list of topics Oprah wants to feature on upcoming shows. If you are having problems with that particular issue, you are invited to e-mail them and share your experience. Kim Crayton noticed that one of the listed topics was indecisiveness. Kim felt she was the Queen of Indecision, as it could take her days to make up her mind. Her motto was, "I'm undecided and that's final."

Kim submitted a story about the time it took her three weeks to decide whether to buy a thirty-dollar purse. Sure enough, she was called to appear on the show and had the opportunity to receive advice from Dr. Phil ("Is that working for you?") that helped her overcome her overanalyzing. As a result, she start offering workshops on how people could reverse their habitual "wishy-washiness." She came up with a great title by asking herself, What's my thought process when I'm trying to make a decision? She realized she went back and forth in her mind wondering, Should I, shouldn't I, should I, shouldn't I? That was it. "Should I, Shouldn't I?" expressed the core of this surprisingly common problem.

PIQUE THEIR CURIOSITY

I think if a mother could ask a fairy godmother to endow her child with the most useful gift, that gift would be curiosity.
ELEANOR ROOSEVELT

This technique can also work well for elevator introductions. If people ask, "What do you do?" and you explain our job at length, they remain in the spectator state. They probably won't absorb or retain what you said and may respond with a polite but passive "oh."

Responding to "What do you do?" with a question means the other person is participating in your intro. By definition they'll be more invested in what you have to offer because they're talking about it in a way that's relevant to them. Furthermore, when they answer your question, they're giving you valuable information. You now know how to tailor what you say next to make sure it's pertinent to their needs, interests, circumstances, or level of familiarity with your work.

Turning your elevator intro into a qualifying question can be particularly important if you work for an obscure company that no one recognizes or if you have a complex job no one understands.

A participant in one of my presentations for the Young Presidents Organization was the founder of a successful software-design company. Unfortunately, when people asked what he did and he tried to explain it, their eyes would glaze over and they would look for any excuse to wander off.

I knew we could develop a more interesting intro if we identified a real-world benefit of his work. I kept asking him, "How does what you do help people do something tangible?" Finally, he mentioned something about computers and credit cards. "Oh," I said, the light bulb finally going on, "did you design a program that makes it possible for people to buy things online with their credit cards?" "Yes!" he said gratefully.

Now when people ask him, "What do you do?" he asks, "Have you ever bought anything from Amazon, Craigslist, or eBay?" (He deliberately names those three companies because millions of people have bought something from those sites, which increases the likelihood they'll feel a connection to his work.) They either say, "Yes" or "Well, not from them, but I pay some of my bills online." He then says, "I make the software that makes it safe for you to use your credit card online." "Aaahh," they say. Believe me, an intrigued "aaahh" is better than an apathetic "oh."

By the way, this is an excellent exercise to do with your staff. Every time your employees introduce themselves in public, they have an opportunity to favorably position your company. At your next staff meeting, ask your colleagues what they say when asked, "What do you do?" You will hear a variety of responses, some good, some not so good. You might want to dedicate part of that meeting to brainstorming possible responses so the next time they're asked "What do you do?" they can respond in a strategic, consistent way that depicts them and your company positively.

HOW TO USE THE POP! THE QUESTION TECHNIQUE

*We should not only master questions, but also
act upon them, and act definitely.*
WOODROW WILSON

Step 1. Review all the possible slogans, pitches, or introductions you've produced so far. Are they declarative statements? If so, ask yourself if phrasing them as questions might do a better job of engaging your target audience's interest.

Step 2. What's your usual response to the question, "What do you do?" or "Why should I buy this?" or "Why should I work with you?" Do you just tell people about your job or offering? What could you ask that would elicit some free information so you could then customize your response?

Step 3. When is the next networking event, business luncheon, or professional meeting you'll be attending? Prepare a variety of elevator introductions and plan on using this as an opportunity to test which receives the best response. Read people's body language and gauge their level of enthusiasm. Which questions do the best job of eliciting genuine intrigue in what you have to offer? Invest some time in fine-tuning your elevator intro so it engages people's curiosity and positions your offering favorably.

Our next technique explains how you can give your product a name that makes it self-explanatory. This is important because most people don't want to work too hard to figure out what your product does. If it's confusing, they're on to the next thing.

Speaking of the next thing. Onward.

14

Make It Sound Like What It Is with OnoNAMEopoeia

If I look confused, it's because I'm thinking.
SAMUEL GOLDWYN

My son Tom, in high school at the time, needed to write an essay about a foreign country. I told him I was going to the grocery store and would be glad to drop him off at the library so he could do his research. He laughed and said, "No thanks, Mom. I'm just going to look it up online."

Gone are the days we need to drive or walk to the library, look up our topic in the card catalog, pull heavy reference books off the shelves, take them back to a table, and pore over them for hours looking for relevant information. Now all we have to do is sit at our computer, type in a key word to our favorite search engine, and everything we need to know is instantly at our fingertips.

We have become accustomed to these miraculous Internet directories and may not give them a second thought. However, when this technology was first founded, Sergey Brin and Larry Page faced a challenge. They knew the name they gave their creation was all-important, as it would form people's perceptions of it. If the name was complicated, people might conclude the process was complicated and steer away from it.

You probably know the end of this story. Brin and Page took their name from the math term *googol*, which is the number 1 followed by 100 zeros. This was a genius move, as *Google* is a playful word that is fun, simple, and easy to say. This is exactly how they wanted their product perceived: fun, simple, and easy to use. Plus, their name represents the trillions of usages they envisioned for their search engine (20,000 uses per *second*, as reported in the November 21 issue of the *Washington Post*).

When we introduce something for the first time, people don't have any frame of reference for it. That means our invention can come across as confusing or intimidating unless we make it self-explanatory. One way to achieve that all-important instant recognition is to give your creation a name that sounds like what it is or does.

Onomatopoeia means "the formation of a word (as in *cuckoo* or *boom*) by imitation of a sound made by or associated with its referent." I took a little poetic license here and riffed off that word to create the technique *OnoNAMEopoeia* which means "to form a name for our offering that imitates the sound, look, or emotion felt when using it."

Another popular Internet directory has an OnoNAMEopoeia name. Let's look at two of its Core Words, *search* and *engine*. Engine is a rather technical word. Engines can be complex. Only mechanics really understand how to make them operate. They could have added a little twist and called their invention *Enginuity*, but that's difficult to spell and could make their process seem daunting rather than doable.

So, let's look at the other Core Word *search*. We've all searched for something or someone. That's an everyday phrase everyone's familiar with and comfortable with. Okay, what do we say when we find what we search for? How about *Yahoo!*? Voilà!

In fact, Yahoo! founders David Filo and Jerry Yang, Ph.D., told Hal Plotkin in Silicon Valley's weekly newspaper, the *Metro*, that this "goofy name has given us a major advantage. It is a pretty recognizable brand name. Originally, it was Jerry's Guide to the World Wide Web, but we settled on Yahoo!, a word we came up with while lampooning the digitalese of the other hierarchically organized lists we'd been looking at. Yahoo! stands for 'Yet Another Hierarchically Organized list.'"

"I was not crazy about the name at first," Filo adds, "but it grew on me. Now I'm grateful my partners selected a name that conveys the sense of fun involved in all this. That is what really distinguishes our site. It is a place for adventures. A place to discover things.'"

GIVE PEOPLE A EUREKA MOMENT

What's another word for thesaurus?
STEPHEN WRIGHT

To arrive at your own OnoNAMEopeia name, all you need to do is get a few friends together and talk out loud about the "audio-visual" characteristics that distinguish you, your brand, or business.

Did you play charades growing up? Remember how the game works? You are given the name of a movie, book, song, or well-known person, and your job is to give visual clues to your teammates until they guess the right name. You can't say the actual word or phrase. You have to act it out, using hand gestures, body language, and enthusiastic nods to let your teammates know when they're getting close. When done right, people finally connect the dots and almost involuntarily shout out the answer because they have that euphoric Eureka Moment when all the clues come together and they get the right answer.

You can crystallize just the right title or tagline for your offering by playing charades, in reverse. Instead of being given the name in advance, you and your colleagues are going to bat questions, Core

Words, and descriptions of your invention back and forth until they, all of a sudden, come together to coin the perfect phrase for your priority project. It may take a while, but if you're patient and keep playing with language options, you will get closer and closer until you "connect the POP!s" and have your own Eureka Moment.

SPEAK YOUR CUSTOMERS' LINGO

There is one thing stronger than all the armies in the world,
and that is an idea whose time has come.
VICTOR HUGO

Another version of this technique is to give your offering a name that sounds like the vernacular spoken by your target audience. If you're marketing to teenagers it has to have a cool name they'd feel comfortable using around their peers, or it won't appeal to them.

Susan Brown, the inventor of the number-one baby product in the country, according to *American Baby* magazine, obviously understood the power of lingo when she came up with one of those "Why didn't I think of that?" inventions.

The manager of the day-care center where Brown took her baby daughter asked her to bring in a pillow so they could prop up her baby, who couldn't yet sit up on her own. Instead of just bringing in a pillow off the bed or couch, Brown's creativity kicked in. Overnight, she thought up and then made up a C-shaped pillow stuffed with foam that made it easier for her baby to sit up. It was an instant hit with the child-care providers and became a multimillion-dollar business. In seventeen years, the basic design hasn't changed, although mothers now use the pillow for a variety of purposes, such as supporting their baby while breast-feeding so their backs and arms don't get too tired.

What did Brown call her handy creation? *Boppy*. An inspired choice. *Boppy* sounds like baby talk. A lot of adults add the *e* sound to words when around infants: *blankie, dolly, nappy. Boppy* illustrates how your product can POP! out when you give it a name that matches the language used by your target audience.

ANYONE CAN BE MORE ORIGINAL

Everyone is a genius at least once a year; a real genius
has his original ideas closer together.
G. C. LICHTENBERG

The artificial intelligence geniuses at iRobot invented a marvelous new device that vacuums your floors for you. It is called "the lazy person's dream product." We have met the future, folks . . . and its name is *Roomba.*

Think about it. This contraption cleans rooms while swiveling and dancing across the floor, much like a rhumba. Like *Google* and *Yahoo!, Roomba* is fun and easy to say, and fun and easy to use.

Not content to stop there, iRobot just released a new product to capitalize on the success of Roomba, which has already sold 1.5 million units. Their new appliance actually has sensors so it doesn't tumble down stairs or get stuck behind hard-to-reach places. The company deliberately selected a name that resembled their original product, while indicating it uses a liquid solution to scrub floors. We give you *Scooba.*

Another version of this technique is to give your creation a name that reflects both what it looks like and how you want people to feel when they're consuming it. What would you call a cereal that was O-shaped and designed to cheer up grumpy early-morning risers? How about *Cheerios?*

HOW TO USE THE ONONAMEOPOEIA TECHNIQUE

*Words fascinate me. They always have. For me, browsing
in a dictionary is like being turned loose in a bank.*
EDDIE CANTOR

Step 1. Review your W9 Form and list of Core Words. Do any of them depict the feeling you want people to have when using your product? What other words capture how you'd like your invention perceived? Roll the possibilities around in your mind and mouth. Play with them to see if you can form them into a name that gives your brand instant recognition because it is the language equivalent of your product's benefits.

Step 2. Embark on a sensory journey of your priority project. What sound does it make when it's being operated? How does it feel when you touch it? What does it look like in motion? Write down your sensory descriptions, even if what you're saying isn't a word in the dictionary. Can you turn that sound into a new word and name for your product? People will relate to it because it's similar to what it looks, sounds, or feels like when they're using it. It's what they already associate with it.

15

Add It Up with Alpha and Omega

A powerful agent is the right word. Whenever we come upon one of those intensely right words, the resulting effect is physical as well as spiritual, and electrically prompt.

MARK TWAIN

Are you an ice cream fan? If so, you can probably remember the first time you went into an ice cream store and discovered "add-ins." I don't know the name of the genius who decided to jazz up vanilla ice cream by folding in M&M's, Oreos, and chocolate chip–cookie dough; however, my hat's off to him or her.

We can learn from that lesson. We can jazz up our language by taking a vanilla word and adding on or adding in partial phrases to invent the next new thing.

For example, what does Disney call its "keep it green" programs that support a commitment to environmental issues? *Environmentality.* That's an Omega (the last letter of the Greek alphabet) word where a suffix was added to the end of the word.

There's a trend now for longtime couples to renew their wedding vows. As a way to show their ongoing commitment, these couples hold a ceremony where they swear in front of God and friends and family that they're going to continue to stay married. What should we call this cultural phenomenon? First, ask yourself, What do they call two people who just got married for the first time? *Newlyweds*, right?

Now, look at the first line of the previous paragraph to find a prefix that could turn this into an intensely right Alpha (the first letter of the Greek alphabet) word that names this cultural phenomenon. There it is. *Renewlyweds*.

ARE YOU LOOKING AT LIFE IN AN UNHABITUAL WAY?

*Genius means little more than the faculty of
perceiving in an unhabitual way.*
WILLIAM JAMES

From now on, when you observe a trend or cultural phenomenon, ask yourself, What can I add to the beginning or end of this word to create a proprietary term? Look at it your Core Words in unhabitual ways to see if you can morph them into a one-of-a-kind phrase.

I was honored to be asked to coordinate the *Creativity Alive* track for the Young Presidents' Organization's 2005 Family University in Ireland. I invited Dave Barry and Ridley Pearson to present an old-fashioned story hour, knowing it would be a perfect program for young and old. You may know Dave as a funny syndicated columnist and Ridley as an award-winning mystery writer. What you may not know is they coauthored a bestselling children's book, *Peter and the Starcatchers*, a prequel to *Peter Pan*.

The two dressed up in pirate gear, complete with pointy hats, kerchiefs, and eye patches. Since both have young children, they knew they needed to get the kids involved, so they tossed out treats to anyone who asked a question. As soon as the kids realized there was candy to be had by simply asking a question, a hundred eager hands shot up in the air. Kids were falling all over themselves to be the next in line.

I bet you can come up with a relevant word for the commotion in the room. What's it called when there's chaos or a ruckus? *Pandemonium*, right? Combine that with a Core Word in their book title and you arrive at a fun Omega phrase: *Peter Pandemonium*.

I've supplied some common prefixes and suffixes below. Add them to the beginning (Alpha) or end (Omega) of your Core Words to transform them into terms you could trademark, own, and turn into a business empire.

Prefixes		Suffixes	
re	multi	ly	ology
pre	dis	ion	ize
non	sub	able	er
un	trans	ith	ish
inter	anti	ous	ate

You don't have to use common prefixes and suffixes for your add-ons. It sometimes works to add a verb to your word that indicates what you want your product to achieve for your customers. For example, a company that makes snoring remedies created a simple but powerful name for their product. What did they want it to do for their customers? *SnoreStop*. You can't get much more direct than that.

What verb captures the action you want your customers to take? What descriptive adjective could you combine with one of your Core Words to coin a phrase that shows exactly what your product does for your customers?

As you can imagine, the shorter the word the better. I think Next Day Blinds is a great name for a company because you know exactly what this company delivers. Add the words below to the beginning or ending of your Core Words to see if you can coin a brand name that captures the essence of what you have to offer. *Stop. Start. Go. Now. Fix. Yes. Self. Super. Fast. Slow. Today. Grow. Master. Best. First. Last. Top.*

JAZZ UP YOUR VANILLA WORDS

A man who works with his hands is a laborer; a man who works
with his hands and his brain is a craftsman; but a man who
works with his hands and his brain and his heart is an artist.
LOUIS NIZER

I am using the word *jazz* deliberately in this chapter. Webster's defines it as "music marked by intricate, propulsive rhythms; polyphonic ensemble playing; improvisatory, virtuosic solos; melodic freedom; and a harmonic idiom ranging from simple diatonicism through chromaticism to atonality." It is also slang for "liveliness, spirit, excitement."

Wow. That's a mouthful. Let's just say jazz is a form of musical creativity. My hope is that POP! is a form of communication creativity.

What jazz musicians do, POP! practitioners do. The best messages are lively and have a musical beat or propulsive rhythm to them. Brainstorming is a form of improvising and frees up the potential for virtuosity in language. We make some of our messages melodic so they have a smooth sound and others deliberately dissonant to cause people to question what they thought they knew. When it all comes together in perfect phrasing, it's sweet music and it is definitely exciting.

HOW TO USE THE TECHNIQUES IN THIS SECTION

I not only use all the brains I have, I use all the brains I can borrow.
CALVIN COOLIDGE

As we wrap up this section, it's a good time to introduce a concept called Buddy Brainstorming that can help you produce even more results from this (and other) exercises. As Coolidge pointed out, why not benefit from the brainpower of others? Ask a friend or associate if he or she would meet with you for an hour so the two of you can develop a POP! title, tagline, or elevator introduction for your priority projects to help them stand out.

Step 1. Go somewhere private so the two of you can concentrate without distraction. Decide who will go first and who will act as scribe. You'll switch roles after the first round so you both get an opportunity to workshop your priority project.

Step 2. Bring out your W9 Form and tell your partner what you'd like to achieve in your thirty minutes. Would you like to win buy-in to a proposal you're presenting? Want to name your business or come up with a great headline?

Step 3. Start with the Alpha and Omega technique. Add the sample prefixes and suffixes on page 137 to each of your Core Words to see if you can produce a proprietary phrase. Brainstorm out loud, verbally playing with possibilities while the scribe takes notes. Please note: The scribe won't be able to get down everything you say unless she or he is a whiz at shorthand. Just try to capture key words that will trigger your memory so you can go back and expand upon it later.

Step 4. When you're about halfway through your time, try one of the other techniques in this section. Maybe you'd like to Alphabetize your Core Words to create some clever variations. Perhaps you can put yourself in the middle of a challenge your customers are facing and talk out loud while the scribe captures the catchphrases that come out of your mouth.

Another note: When generating possibilities, say whatever comes to mind, without judgment. If you slow down, it means you're overthinking and evaluating whether this idea will work. In the brainstorming process, everything counts. As James Thurber said, "Don't get it right, just get it written." Your goal right now is to create, not to criticize. The more options, the better. Draft now, craft later.

Step 5. When you have five minutes left in your time, review what you've produced and pick what POP!s out. Remember, what catches *your* attention will often catch other people's attention.

This is an enormously satisfying part of the POP! process. As E. M. Forster said, "How can I know what I think until I hear what I say?" Having an opportunity to immerse yourself in your topic and explore options (without censure) can help you achieve an exquisite state of flow in which you are lost in thought. You may not even remember what you said, which makes it fascinating to review the notes with fresh eyes and ears. It's as if you're hearing these ideas for the first time. In a way, you are.

Be sure to explore "tip of the iceberg" ideas. When you both find an idea particularly intriguing, spend more time on it. Explain and expand upon what you mean by it. Tip of the iceberg ideas are like great art in that they work on a lot of levels. The longer you look at them, the deeper you think about them, the more they reveal.

Resist the urge to switch back and forth and brainstorm both of your projects at once. There's no substitute for submerging yourself in one subject. It's a rare opportunity to be selfish and to talk at length about something you care about. The point of this exercise is to comprehensively explore your offering. There is a cumulative mental momentum when you're allowed to run with your thoughts instead of having to arbitrarily cut them off to give the other person his or her turn.

Step 6. At the end of thirty minutes, it's time to switch turns and give your partner a chance to brainstorm his or her idea, slogan, or message. Enjoy!

In the next section, you'll learn the art and science of how to condense your message into a sound bite that says a lot in a little.

FOUR

Be PITHY

I try to leave out the parts people skip.

ELMORE LEONARD

16

Make Your Language Lyrical with Alliteration

Your opening has to be good—or the rest of the story won't have a chance because nobody'll stick around to read it.

LAWRENCE BLOCK

B lock is right. The beginning of our message better be good, and *short*, or people won't hang around to hear the rest of it.

Remember in Chapter 1, I mentioned the mind can only hold seven bits of information in short-term memory, so it's our job to make a long story short? This section provides three specific ways we can craft succinct sound bites that POP! The first way is to use alliteration.

Jamie Allison, a mother from Santa Barbara, California, decided to get back into shape in 1999 so she could "look better, feel better, have more energy, and get that flushed face, that glow." She knew it's often tough to go it alone so she formed a support group with other women who wanted to train for triathalons. She could have called the group something like FTT (Females Training for Triathalons), but that's not very likable or memorable. Instead Jamie came up with the name Moms in Motion with an accompanying motto of "fun, fitness, philanthropy." That alliterative, approachable name may be one of the reasons they now have chapters in thirty cities across the country.

ALLITERATION CAN MAKE YOU INSTANTLY ELOQUENT

Word-carpentry is like any other kind of carpentry:
you must join your sentences smoothly.
ANATOLE FRANCE

Say these words. *Bed, Bath and Beyond. Dunkin' Donuts. Rolls Royce.*

Now, say *Bed, Shower, and Powder Room. Dunkin' Croissants. Rolls Jaguar.*

Not the same, is it? Alliteration, words that start with the same sound, is pleasing to the mind and ear. It gives our message a musical lilt, an appealing harmony that makes it feel correct and complete. Perhaps most importantly, alliteration gives our mind a hook on which to hang a memory.

Once you've drafted your title, tagline, or elevator intro, play with the words to make them alliterative. Take the nonessential words and replace them with synonyms that start with the same sound as your Core Word. Keep switching words with meaningful substitutes until the right phrasing falls into place.

You know you've come up with a POP! title or tagline when you wouldn't change a word. There's a feel to an ideal name and slogan. You know it's right as soon as you hear it or see it. You have no compulsion to fiddle with it. It's perfect the way it is.

Just as certain people have chemistry, certain phrases have chemistry. Alliteration leads to "communication chemistry" because it represents a level of craftsmanship that makes your language resonate. Instead of just being a harsh, haphazard mix of words, it transcends into the smooth-sounding language equivalent of a word symphony.

Alliteration can also help your phrasing POP! off the page and

POP! into people's minds. Look at these well-known names and notice how they feel finished.

King Kong
Boombox
Weight Watchers
Dirt Devil
Best Buy
Circuit City

CREATE IDEA EQUITY

Money to a writer is time to write.
FRANK HERBERT

Do you have a favorite place to stop on your way to work to get a morning cup of coffee, espresso, or latté? Chances are, you use one of those little cardboard holders to keep from burning your fingers. Did you know those little cardboard holders are a multimillion-dollar industry?

They seem pretty standard, don't they? There doesn't appear to be anything special about them. Any paper company could manufacture them, right? Try telling that to the creator of *Java Jacket*. Jay Sorenson gave his creation an alliterative name that has helped turn it into a name brand that has cornered the market and made him a lot of money in the process ($15 million in annual revenues, at last report).

More importantly, Jay says, "Java Jacket is a perfect name because it describes what our product does and it is a name customers remember. It has such a dominating market awareness that sometimes people who meant to call our competitors call us instead.

The trademarked Java Jacket name is worth more than our patents."

To an entrepreneur, money means you've produced a valuable item or idea that gives you the freedom to do what you love while getting paid for it. This hinges on you giving your invention a singular name that helps it command mind share and market share. You can charge more for something that has an identity. If your product is perceived as being generic, you can't own it in the public's mind.

If people can't (or don't) refer to your product by a specific name, it's seen as a stock item that doesn't really belong to anyone or have any distinguishing characteristics that make it better than the rest. Only when you attach a recognizable proper name to something, does it turn into Idea Equity, an identifiable brand you can register, own, and profit from for years to come.

A participant in one of my seminars asked, "Sam, do all of our titles, taglines, and elevator introductions need to be alliterative? I am an accountant who speaks and writes primarily to fellow CPAs. Sometimes they're turned off by language they perceive to be contrived or cutesy."

I told him, "Good point. If, in your judgment, alliteration makes your phrasing feel forced or false, don't use it. As my friend Mariah reminds me, 'Never sacrifice clear for clever.' If it sounds over the top and you're afraid it will alienate your target audience, toss it."

Remember, POP! communication is supposed to be purposeful. If you are writing or speaking to a business group, and you anticipate they will perceive your approach or language as being simplistic or touchy-feeling, then change it to something that will maintain your credibility with your intended readers and listeners.

HOW TO USE THE ALLITERATION TECHNIQUE

At first it's a bit jagged, awkward, but then there's a point where there's a click and you suddenly become quite fluent.
DORIS LESSING

Ready to create your own fluent phrases that have a musicality that can make them more appealing and memorable?

Step 1. Bring out your Core Words. Also bring out any notes you might have with potential titles, taglines, and elevator introductions.

Step 2. Look at your draft phrase or sentence. What word has to stay for it to maintain its meaning? What words can't or don't you want to take out because they are crucial to getting your point across? Those are your keeper words.

Step 3. Now, play with the other words, one by one, in your message to see if you can make them alliterative. Look up synonyms to find words that retain your meaning but start with the same sound as your keeper words.

Step 4. If switching the words around doesn't produce an option that's a fluent fit, check out synonyms for your keeper words. Maybe you can substitute something that works just as well but gives you a better option. Persist until word combinations that were jagged or awkward all of a sudden click.

17

Put Your Slogan in a Beat That's Easy to Repeat

"It Don't Mean a Thing If It Ain't Got That Swing"
DUKE ELLINGTON SONG TITLE

Have you seen the TV commercial featuring Peter Boyle and Doris Roberts from *Everybody Loves Raymond* that shows Peter sitting on the edge of his bed in his pajamas, holding his stomach and groaning, "I can't believe I ate the whole thing."

Why is Alka-Seltzer reusing a slogan they first introduced decades ago? It consists, primarily, of one-syllable words, which makes it simple to remember. It's said with a distinctive inflection, "I can't be-*lieve* I ate the whooooole thing," which makes it easy to repeat. When we hear a slogan that's said with a distinctive and exaggerated intonation, we are more likely to mimic that intonation when we see it and say it, which brands that product slogan in our mind and in the public's collective consciousness.

Furthermore, most of us can feel his pain. At one time or another, we've probably had eyes bigger than our stomachs so we've experienced a similar discomfort. No one has to explain what he means. We've been there, felt that.

And this slogan is packaged into a pithy sound bite, one of several reasons it has stood the test of time. Can you craft your slogan so it's phrased in a beat that's easy to repeat? Can you give it a distinctive, exaggerated intonation so people are likely to say it the same way you did?

You may be familiar with Verizon's slogan, "Can you hear me now?" Those five words aren't anything special—until you repeat them in the signature style featured in all their TV and radio commercials. The phrase has become ubiquitous, and not just because Verizon has paid millions of dollars to imprint it in the public's mind and memory.

Why does it help to put our slogans in a specific cadence? Think back to kindergarten and first grade. Do you remember learning such childhood verses as "Jack and Jill went up the hill to fetch a pail of water. Jack fell down and broke his crown . . ."? Nursery rhymes are often taught in a musical cadence because they're easier to replicate and remember.

If you were given a string of twenty-six letters and told you had to remember and recite them, all in the proper order, you would probably say, "No way."

Yet you were able to do just that by putting the alphabet into an iambic rhythm: *a-b-c-d, e-f-g, h-i-j-k, l-m-n-o-p*. Stressing and then unstressing certain words turns this into an easy-to-remember-and-repeat song.

CREATE A DISTINCTIVE CADENCE

*Grammar is a piano I play by ear. All I know
about grammar is its power.*
JOAN DIDION

An *iamb* is defined by Webster's as "a foot of two syllables, a short followed by a long in quantitative meter, or an unstressed followed by a stressed in accentual meter, as 'Come live / with me / and be / my love.'"

Now that we've got that cleared up. Ahem. We don't have to get too technical about this. My editor, Marian Lizzi, told me she was always told to think of iambic meter as when we accent every other beat as in "Ta DUM, ta DUM, ta DUM, ta DUM, ta DUM."

I agree with Joan Didion and ask that we play this one by ear rather than getting too strict. Our goal is simply to experiment with the emphasis and accent on our phasing until it falls into a satisfying rhythmical rightness.

If you were born in the 1950s or 1960s, you can probably fill in these once-popular jingles, "Mmm, mmm, good. Mmm, mmm, good. That's what _____ soup is, mmm, mmm good." Did you supply the word Campbell's? Another timeless slogan (so to speak) is for Timex: "It takes a licking and keeps on _____." Did you say *ticking*?

How about "Double your pleasure, double your fun with Doublemint, Doublemint, Doublemint gum." There's a *lot* right with this jingle. First, the product name is inserted in the slogan, which means it's imprinted on your mind every time you hear or see it. It has a near rhyme (fun and gum) at the end of the two-part phrasing, and it doubles up on the word *double* so it's an actual play on words. Perhaps most importantly, it features a raplike rhythm that acts like an "ear worm," a catchy jingle we can't get out of our heads.

Think about what just happened. You probably hadn't heard or seen these commercials or slogans in (gulp) many years, yet you were able to repeat them word for word, probably in their original singsong beat. That's why it's worth crafting your message until it has a distinctive tempo that can help you establish and imprint recognition for your brand . . . even decades later.

Dr. Phil, he of the "What's Your Guy Q?" tagline, just came out with a book called *Smart Love*. The iambic tagline is "Find the one you want. Fix the one you've got." You can almost tap your foot to that subtitle. Notice he used a contraction. Why? Try saying that subtitle with the words *you have* instead of *you've*. Hear how it complicates the cadence? It sounds better with *you've* because it keeps each word one syllable and maintains the melody. You know it's complete when it's got that beat.

WORDS THAT ROLL OFF THE TONGUE STAY IN THE BRAIN

> *If you have an important point to make, don't try to be subtle or clever. Use a pile driver. Hit the point once. Then come back and hit it again. Then hit it a third time—a tremendous whack.*
> WINSTON CHURCHILL

Perhaps one of the most dramatic examples of the power of a crafted sound bite was demonstrated by the late Johnnie Cochran, one of the defense lawyers for O. J. Simpson. After nine months of testimony from dozens of experts and witnesses, Cochran wrapped up the lengthy, complex trial of the century with a rhythmic phrase that many legal analysts claim won the case.

His summation, of course, was "If it doesn't fit, you must acquit."

I'm not commenting on the innocence or guilt of O. J. Simpson. It's just that after hundreds of hours of evidence, this sound bite is what the jurors remembered of everything they'd heard. In fact, years later, I can describe this scenario to a room full of people in one of my POP! presentations, and when I ask participants if they recall the phrase I'm talking about, most of them can repeat it verbatim.

When you examine this iconic phrase, which CourtTV.com said was originated by another member of the defense dream team, you begin to appreciate its genius. The phrase Cliff Noted and Aflac'd the lengthy trial into a seven-word sound bite that demonstrated O.J.'s innocence. (I know, I know. Many people believe O.J. exaggerated the difficulty of putting on the glove.)

Furthermore, under the law, where reasonable doubt exists, the jury *must* acquit. The purpose then of Cochran's summation was to drive that point home with a pile driver. By deliberately placing the crucial word last in the phrase, by doubling its voice value by trading off the previous word rhyme *fit*, and by saying *acquit* with forceful emphasis, he succeeded in doing just that.

Of all the things Johnnie Cochran could have said to try to establish doubt in the jurors' minds, he selected a phrase that recalled a visual demonstration they could *see* in their minds and reinforced that image with a rhythmically structured phrase that made it easy to repeat and remember. It is a testimony to the far-reaching impact of a well-crafted message.

Please read the next sentence out loud until it falls into a rhythm. *It's Hard to Make a Difference When You Can't Find Your Keys.* Isn't that evocative? This book by Marilyn Byfield Paul could have been called something routine like *Organize Your Stuff*, but instead she opted for a high-concept title that focused on a common dilemma. Instead of describing nitty-gritty details, high-concept titles take the "helicopter" view and explain the overarching premise of your project, whether it's a movie, book, or campaign. Marilyn had noticed that many people wanted to lead a life that mattered, but they were overwhelmed with the minutia of life and too busy with everyday tasks. Once Marilyn came up with that altruistic goal of clearing away clutter to free time for higher-priority projects, she was able to craft a rhythmical title that was sublime.

INFLECTION CAN HELP MAKE
YOUR MESSAGE POP!

The art of art, the glory of expression, and the sunshine
of the light of letters is simplicity.
WALT WHITMAN

Once you craft your sound bite into a cadence, it's important to say it with the same inflection, every time, so it's turned into a signature line that is associated only with you.

A famous radio broadcaster is known for a segment of his show called "And now, for the *rest* of the story!" and for the distinctive way he closes his show, "This is Paul Harvey. Good *day!*" He says these simple words with the same distinctive lilt every single time. People recognize them as *his* lines. That's branding.

No doubt you've heard the popular phrase "Let's get ready to rumble." American boxing announcer Michael Buffer has actually trademarked that catchphrase. That's right. If you use his distinctive version of those five words, you have to get permission and pay him royalties. His inimitable take on that expression has been used extensively to hype sports events, has been featured in a video game, and was the main lyric in his hit single. Really. That's the power of using exaggerated inflection to turn an everyday phrase into *your* phrase.

Chandler Bing, Matthew Perry's character on the hit sitcom *Friends*, was famous for putting an unusual emphasis on the word *be*. He would say, "Could you *be* any more rude?" "Could this *be* any stranger?" Such a little thing. Such a *big* difference.

Fans could easily mimic Chandler (and did) because of his distinctive inflection. What's the value of that, you ask? The goal of a show is to have viewers IMing each other with the latest development and talking about last night's episode around the watercooler.

When you are motivated and able to repeat a standout line you've heard only once, that turns you into a word-of-mouth ambassador for that show. People who had never seen *Friends* heard the water-cooler conversation about what Chandler said the night before and were inspired to tune in to the next episode, all because the writers and Matthew Perry gave his communication a vocal flair that helped it stand out.

HOW TO PUT YOUR SLOGAN IN A BEAT THAT'S EASY TO REPEAT

There's a kind of ear music . . . a rhythmic synchronicity which creates a kind of heartbeat on the page.
ALLAN GURGANUS

Ready to craft your message into a distinctive rhythm so it's easier to remember?

Step 1. This technique works better when you have a friend help you tap out a percussive rhythm. Partner with a pal and read your Core Words and potential slogans out loud while your friend taps out a metronome beat. Fran Lebowitz said, "When I write, I read everything out loud to get the right rhythm." Be sure to test potential POP! messages by saying them out loud. Tap your foot (as a musician would to maintain the beat) and try to fit the words of your marketing message into a specific cadence.

Step 2. If the phrasing doesn't fall into an easy-to-repeat beat, experiment with some of your other Core Words to see and hear if any have the right synchronicity. Perhaps you can "pull a Chandler" and put an unexpected emphasis on a word that catches people by surprise and becomes your signature saying.

Step 3. Try expanding or shortening your phrase. Experiment with contractions to see if that makes your message flow off the tongue and stay in the brain. Think of this as the language equivalent of a musical score. Keep playing with the inflection and tempo until the word pieces fall into place and there's an easy feel and rhythmic rightness to your message. If you want a specific idea to POP! off the page, feature alliterative words with hard consonants (such as the letters *k*, *p*, or *t*) that hit on the *ta DUM* so you're punching your key point in a forceful way that drives your message home.

18

Make It Sublime with Rhyme

Language is half art, half instinct.
CHARLES DARWIN

If you've ever taken a workshop on teamwork or leadership, you've probably heard of or experienced Dr. Bruce Tuckman's 1965 model of team development and group process. He identified four steps to acquiring skills and adopting new habits. Not content to give this four-part process any old name, he called the series of steps "Forming, Storming, Norming, Performing."

Forming is when you come together, *Storming* is when you encounter the difficulties that arise when learning something new, *Norming* is when you establish the systems and routines to do this task, and *Performing* is when you've mastered the fundamentals and are operating naturally and effectively.

Why is his system so widely used and recognized? In my opinion, it's because he condensed his concept into four steps that were labeled with rhyming words that made his language proprietary and memorable. Imagine if he had called his four-part methodology "Gather Together as a Group, Experience Problems and Challenges, Design your Rituals and Patterns, Operate Effectively and Productively." Yikes! Who can remember that? Who wants to?

Abby Marks-Beale, an expert on speed-reading, told me her corporate clients reported their employees were spending up to six hours a day online. They wanted her to develop a new program and book so people could be more efficient when sending computer messages and using the Internet.

Her initial title, *Read More, Faster: Increase Your Effectiveness on the Computer While Reducing Stress and Wasted Effort*, didn't ring or resonate. Abby knew it was important to keep playing with the words until her title POP!ed. After trying a lot of combinations, she came up with *Increasing Productivity Online While Saving Frustration, Time, and Paper.*

Still not very catchy, is it? Let's continue with the trial-and-error experimenting. Let's switch those words around in the subtitle. Hey, how about *Increasing Productivity Online While Saving Paper, Frustration, and Time*. Hear how the near rhyme of *online* and *time* made her language puzzle fall into place? Rearranging the words until they "fit" changed the rhythm and turned a flat title into a fluent title.

You may be thinking that's not a very jazzy title. You're right, it's not. However, Abby's target market is corporate executives and managers. She knows they won't pay for "fluff" programs that come across as touchy-feely. This straightforward title was likely to appeal to them because it focused on delivering bottom-line results and measurable improvement in productivity and profits.

IT COULD BE VERSE

I've known all my life that I could take a bunch of words and throw them up in the air and they would come down just right.
TRUMAN CAPOTE

Good for Capote. For most of us, coming up with the "just right" title, tagline, or elevator intro takes longer. It's worth the effort though because when we structure our message into words that rhyme, our message will be remembered over time.

If I asked you to think of the two instinctive human responses to danger, you might dredge up something you first heard decades ago in school: *fight or flight*. Part of why that phrase is so memorable is because it Cliff Notes an entire concept into a tight sound bite featuring two rhyming words.

REPEATING THE SAME WORD CAN IMPRINT YOUR MESSAGE

Watch children at play. The same is true with writing:
you get caught up in the rhythm. That's when
it really gets to be complete play.
MADELEINE L'ENGLE

It can also be smart to repeat your Core Word at the end of the first and second stanzas of your message. Technically, this is not a rhyme, but it can have the same impact of a rhyme because it sounds the same and "punches" your priority word.

Several years ago the City of Baltimore was looking for a new slogan. This is not trivial. The convention and meeting industry is a $122 billion (yes, that's a *b* as in *big bucks*) industry nationally. Cities and states compete for lucrative convention contracts and tourist dollars with slogans that capitalize on their unique benefits. For example, San Diego showcases its sunny climate with "Come for the convention. Stay for the vacation." New Jersey's acting governor just rejected a slogan his state's task force had already paid $260,000 for. He wasn't convinced the motto "New Jersey: We'll win you over" would deliver on its promise.

The City of Baltimore figured it was time to chuck its current motto, "The City That Reads" (oh, that'll bring 'em in), with something that showcases the city more compellingly. It is financing this project to the tune of a half million dollars and has formed a repositioning task force that has held meetings with city leaders to identify the "personality" of the area.

In my opinion, a good slogan for the city would be "You Get More . . . in Baltimore."

Now, that is not fancy. However, it would imprint the name of the city *and* its benefits every time it's said or read. This would position the city in a meaningful way for their target audience. When meeting planners consider where to hold their next event, when visitors are trying to decide where to spend some free time, this slogan might pull them in because it sells the fact that they'd be getting *more* by choosing Balti*more*.

More of what? you might ask. That's when the marketing department could tailor Baltimore's ads and brochures to itemize how meeting planners and visitors would get *more* for their money, *more* waterfront, *more* history, *more* nightlife, *more* culture, *more* shopping, and so forth.

I'm partial; however, I think the above slogan is enduring and purposeful. The intentional repetition of *more* plays off the city's name and brands it in a way that helps it stand out from all other choices. Hmm, maybe I should call the Baltimore City Council.

Total System Services has been the leading processor of credit cards for twenty years. When you swipe your credit card at a terminal, its technology makes it possible for it to be quickly checked and approved. While the company is invisible to consumers, it is well-known by major credit card issuers. Its slogan showcases the intentional repetition of their key word, "We're the *action* behind the trans*action*."

Look at your last name. Could it also work as an adjective that describes your services? Does it end with a partial phrase you could repeat in your slogan and/or tie back into your topic? If so, you too can brand your name onto your customers' consciousness. Debra

Fine is an expert on conversation and a practitioner of this technique. Her latest book is titled *The Fine Art of Small Talk*.

Popular sportswriter Rick Reilly, author of *Who's Your Caddy?* (a POP! the Question title), also wrote a memoir chronicling his experiences covering world-class athletes. His four-word title contains his last name and another word that's used in the first sentence of this paragraph. Got it? Yup. *The Life of Reilly*. It works on several levels because it's a catchphrase that plays off his name and refers to the remarkable life he's led. Well done.

ANDY WARHOL WAS RIGHT

I see but one rule: to be clear.
STENDAHL

When it comes to POP!, I see *two* rules: be clear and be *compelling*. Andy Warhol said everyone will eventually get fifteen minutes of fame. Due to the remote control, constant channel surfing, and shortened attention spans, I think it's actually closer to fifteen *seconds* these days.

Joe Medeiros, a writer and producer for *The Tonight Show with Jay Leno*, travels around the country visiting invention conventions, gift shows, and trade fairs, filming people pitching their products. He then picks the "best of the best" and shows them on a segment called "Pitch to America." Audience members vote with applause after each pitch to indicate whether they think the product was "Sold or Unsold."

Joe brought his crew to the 2005 Maui Writers Conference. As one of the event organizers, I walked over to their set to make sure Joe had everything he needed. Well, they had everything they needed, except people who were willing to pitch. Seems our attendees were feeling a little shy, so I jumped in front of the cameras to kick-start the process. Thankfully, I had a pitch for my book *Tongue Fu!* that I had polished over the years for radio and TV interviews. Here it is, word for word:

> My name is Sam Horn. (Pause.)
> I've written a book on how to deal with difficult people—without becoming one yourself. (Pause.)
> It's called . . . *Tongue Fu!* (Big smile.)
> Tongue Fu! is . . . martial arts for the mouth. (Point to mouth.)
> Some of the chapters include:
> Fun Fu!—how to handle hassles with humor instead of harsh words,
> Tongue Sue!—Tongue Fu! for lawyers,
> And Run Fu!—for when Tongue Fu! doesn't work.

The Tonight Show producers called a month later to let me know they'd selected my pitch to lead the on-air segment. Why was it chosen to be featured out of the hundreds filmed that weekend? It practiced what POP! teaches.

If you read that pitch out loud, you'll see it is fifteen seconds long and has no superfluous words. It follows E. B. White's advice to "make every word tell."

I paused at the end of each sentence so the audience could clearly hear what was said. Comedians know that the best way to add power to a punch line is to pause dramatically *before* it to elicit anticipation, and to pause *after* it so listeners have time to absorb it. Some people are so nervous when pitching, they talk a mile a minute and their words run together. Arthur Levine, the Scholastic editor for J. K. Rowling's Harry Potter books, once told me, "Sam, I love the way you speak. You put space around your words."

I deliberately said the line "How to deal with difficult people—without becoming one yourself " in a distinctive rhythm so it had a little rock 'n' roll to it. The title *Tongue Fu!* is original, which means it piqued people's curiosity.

"Martial arts for the mouth" is alliterative so it gave people a hook on which to hang this memory. Plus, pointing to my mouth Aflac'd the pitch and helped people see what I was saying so my rhetoric became visual.

Fun Fu!, *Tongue Sue!*, and *Run Fu!* employ the "power of three," a device orators use to expand a theme by sharing three resonant examples. People tend to remember things that come in threes (for example, "Three Little Pigs") because they have a rhythmic beat.

And finally, the playful tone gave the impression the book is fun. Taking ourselves too seriously when pitching can be a fatal flaw. Overearnest explanations give the impression our work could be dull. This is the equivalent of taking literary cod oil. People won't voluntarily buy something that may be good for them but sounds boring.

Did the audience guess it was sold? Overwhelmingly.

As a result of that appearance on *The Tonight Show*, thousands visited our website, signed up for our e-zine, downloaded articles, bought CDs and books, and requested information about my workshops. The book's Amazon.com ranking shot up. Furthermore, millions more people now know about *Tongue Fu!* They may buy it the next time they walk into a bookstore, hire me to speak at an upcoming convention, or arrange for one of our certified Tongue Fu! trainers to teach their employees how to get along better with just about anyone, anytime, anywhere. All because I had a Purposeful, Original, Pithy pitch that got people's favorable attention. That's the power of POP!

HOW TO CREATE A MEMORABLE SOUND BITE

Anybody can make the simple complicated.
Creativity is making the complicated simple.
CHARLES MINGUS

Here's where you put it all together to condense what could be a complicated message into an AIRtight sound bite (Alliteration, Inflection, Rhyme) that imprints your primary point in an unforgettable way.

Step 1. Write down your best option for your pitch, concept, or message. Have you crafted the words so at least two of them are alliterative? If not, do that now.

Step 2. Do you have at least two words that rhyme (for example, *shop* till you *drop*)? If so, great. If not, experiment with synonyms until at least two of your main words sound similar so you have a sublime word symphony that makes your message flow.

Step 3. Is your slogan in a beat that's easy to repeat? If not, start switching the order of the words until the sounds fall into place and your phrase has a distinctive cadence.

Step 4. Practice saying your signature line with varying types of inflection. Accent different words and say your phrase in an unexpected way. Play with an up-and-down musical-scale intonation until you create a brilliant one-liner that will brand itself onto your target audience's minds . . . in a good way.

FIVE

Continue to POP!: Seven Secrets to Keeping Their Interest Once You've Got It

My job is to talk; your job is to listen. If you finish first, please let me know.

HARRY HERSCHFIELD

19

Make Your Content Come Alive with First-Person Stories

The world is not made up of atoms, it's made up of stories.
MURIEL RUKEYSER

A woman in a workshop approached me after a POP! presentation and said, "Okay, you've taught us how to capture people's attention in sixty seconds or less. Now I want to know, how can we keep their attention once we've got it?"

Good question. Have you ever read the classic children's book *The Velveteen Rabbit?* In it, a stuffed horse shows his best friend, a stuffed rabbit, that it doesn't matter if you are raggedy; what matters is if someone loves you. If someone loves you, then you transcend being a thing; you become "alive."

IS YOUR CONTENT LIFELESS OR LIVELY?

I have found that if you love life, life will love you back.
ARTHUR RUBENSTEIN

SpeakerNetNews cofounder Rebecca Morgan had us on the edges of our seats, telling us about a visit to a local mall. "I was walking through the food court and an employee with a plate of orange-spiced chicken approached and asked, 'Want a free sample?' I told him, 'No thanks,' and kept walking.

"Well, I tried to keep walking but he was insistent and said, 'Come on, it's really good.' I told him I didn't want any, but he didn't give up. He actually stepped in front of me, thrust the tooth-picked sample toward my face and said, 'Just one bite?' I finally told him, '*No!*' I almost had to push him aside to get by. I was so annoyed, I vowed never to eat at that place.

"Later, I was on my way out when an indescribably delicious smell stopped me in my tracks. I turned around to see where it was coming from and saw a store across the way with fresh-baked chocolate-chip cookies displayed on the counter. Unable to resist, I retraced my steps and bought a couple to take home with me."

Rebecca then segued into "Chocolate-Chip Cookie Marketing": the anti-hard-sell approach that attracts customers by showing what you have to offer and letting them decide to do business with you.

It was brilliant. She could have launched into her talk with rhetoric (such as "People don't like a hard sell. They're offended when we force our products on them. They often swear never to work with us because they don't like pushy salespeople who try to make their decisions for them"). Blah, blah, blah. Instead, she told a first-person story that made her message come alive in an appealing and memorable way.

Ideas are great, but they're intellectual concepts. That means they can be lifeless because they literally don't have living, breathing human beings in them. Stories that feature people talking and interacting make our material, literally and figuratively, full of life. Ergo, if you want your material to come alive, include first-person stories.

TURN RHETORIC INTO REAL LIFE

Reality leaves a lot to the imagination.
JOHN LENNON

A reporter recently asked me, "What's the *most* important lesson you've learned from your twenty-five years as a professional speaker who's paid to present to organizations?"

I didn't even have to think about it. I said, "Without a first-person story, it's all rhetoric."

Looking puzzled, he asked, "What do you mean?"

I smiled because, in a weird kind of way, he had just proved my point. He had asked a question and I had given an answer that, in my experience, is profound, yet for him it was theoretical and had no meaning. He couldn't relate to what I had just said and certainly didn't feel any passion for it.

The secret to keeping people's attention is simple. Stories. Not just any kind of story. There's a system for crafting and telling a story that makes it come alive. I'll share that system in the next chapter. First, an example . . .

Do you see what just happened?

I introduced a concept in the last few paragraphs. You may have been nodding your head and thinking, That makes sense. Or, I understand that. At this point, you were observing what was being said and deciding whether this was news to you or already in your bank of knowledge.

This evaluative process goes on constantly when you're reading, watching, and listening. The problem is, this process is temporary and fleeting. You're processing information but not giving your mind a way to retain it. Unless you switch your brain from passively observing to personally relating to how you could use that information, you won't own it. The idea remains the author's or speaker's . . . not yours.

Your mind is bombarded with so much data that it decided a long time ago it couldn't store it all. So it filters the data and only retains information that is dramatically personally relevant or what we consciously tell it to remember.

Uh-oh. More expository rhetoric. See, I keep trying to explain this idea to you and just keep piling words on top of each other. At this point, instead of "getting" what I'm saying, you may be getting tired of it. Your head is hearing it, but your heart's not into it.

You may be thinking of the famous "Yada, yada, yada" episode of *Seinfeld*. You may even start skimming the book (or if I was speaking, you'd start studying the inside of your eyelids) because you'd feel I was taking way too long to get to the point.

This all changes, though, as soon as we say, "For example." That's when "thinks" get interesting, original, and real life. That's when they get to the point. That's when our imagination kicks in. If you really want to shake people out of their reverie and motivate them to sit up and take notice, say those two simple words, *for example*.

EXAMPLES ARE BETTER THAN EXPLANATIONS

The idea is to write it so that people hear it and it slides through the brain and goes straight to the heart.
MAYA ANGELOU

So, what's your story? Why did you create this product? How did you start your business? Where were you and what were you doing when you came up with this idea? People like to know where things come from. Once they understand your offering's history or learn about its roots, they feel connected to it and you. You and your offering are no longer inanimate, abstract, or impersonal. *They know your story.*

- Did your invention come to you in a dream? While walking? While brainstorming?
- Did you have a loved one who suffered because they didn't know this or have this, and you want to save others from that pain?
- Did this message gain critical mass over the years as you accumulated observations and then a pivotal event compelled you to share it with others?
- Did you see people doing something counterproductive and you just had to reach out to them and say, "No, please, there's an easier way"?
- Did you design this tool because the normal one is clumsy and awkward to use?
- Do you believe passionately in this campaign and want everyone to vote for this candidate because you know her personally and you can vouch for her integrity?
- Why can you not rest until you act on this and make it a reality?
- Explain why this is important to you, why you're driven to do this, and why you're the best individual or only organization who is satisfactorily dealing with this.

I wrote part of this book at the Seven Springs Ski Resort in Pennsylvania. The management is obviously proud of their heritage and prominently displays photos of their founders around the property. The history of the log buildings, along with the original vision and mission of the family who built it from scratch, are printed on the back of restaurant menus and in a pamphlet distributed to all guests upon check-in. Sharing their behind-the-scenes story gives their hotel a soul that fosters customer loyalty. I felt connected to this destination because I knew its history and roots. It was no longer just another in a string of faceless hotels; it had a personality that made me want to go back and recommend it to others.

Stories transcend rhetoric because they cause us to "see" what's being said, which means we're emotionally engaged. We're not just listening to words, we're imagining what we're hearing or reading as if it's a movie in our mind. That's why we love stories. Whether we're sitting around the campfire, hearing a bedtime story, or listening to a visionary leader at a business conference, stories have the power to draw us together as a community and transport us into a world of collective consciousness.

WHY STORIES ARE THE BEST WAY TO GET YOUR MESSAGE ACROSS

What really happens is the story-maker proves
a successful "subcreator." He makes a secondary
world which your mind can enter.
J.R.R. TOLKIEN

When we are completely swept up with a story, we aren't even aware of the passage of time or conscious of our surroundings. We are one with the storyteller and living in the subworld he or she has created for us.

That is one reason why illustrating each idea with a real-life story is so crucial. It takes people out of their critical left brain and switches them into their emotionally engaged right brain. They are no longer on the outside judging your idea; they are inside experiencing it. That's the essence of buy-in.

You may be wondering how this applies to the work world. Simply said, whether you are addressing employees at a staff meeting or writing an article for an internal newsletter, whether people buy what you're saying or selling depends on whether you back it up with a relevant example that proves your point and demonstrates precedence.

FEATURE ORIGINAL STORIES

*When I go to the movies, one of my strongest desires is to
be shown something new. I want to go to new places,
meet new people, have new experiences. When I see
Hollywood formulas mindlessly repeated, a little
something dies inside of me: I have lost two hours to boors
who insist on telling me stories I have heard before.*

ROGER EBERT

When I say *story*, I don't mean a "it was a dark and stormy night"
story or *someone else's* story. Those have been told before.

I mean an original story that happened to you or someone you've
met or interviewed. I mean a story that emanates from your own experience or features a real person your target audience can relate to.

Start collecting first-person stories that pertain to your topic and
priority project. If something happens to or around you that would
illustrate or prove your point, write it down. Be sure to capture the
dialogue and sensory details so you can make it come alive for your
listeners, readers, or viewers.

Interview peers and members of your profession about your
topic. Interview everyday people in universal types of jobs, like
waiters, department store and grocery store clerks, barbers and
beauty salon operators, taxi drivers, etc. Ask if they've been in
the situation you're focusing on. Ask them to relive what it was
like for them to experience that. What were they thinking, saying, feeling? What were their subsequent lessons learned, insights,
advice?

This is how you gather and generate proprietary intellectual capital that is yours and yours alone. You won't have to worry about disap-
pointing audiences who have heard this material before. You can be
proud of the fact that your Tell 'n Sell anecdotes originated with you.

FEATURE HERO'S JOURNEY STORIES

*Under the ruse of giving an academic lecture, I was trying
to put myself in a bottle that would one day wash up on
the beach for my children.*

RANDY PAUSCH, AUTHOR OF *THE LAST LECTURE*

(WITH JEFFREY ZASLOW)

Joseph Campbell described the classic "Hero's Journey" story as one in which a protagonist leaves home, goes out in the world, encounters a challenge, prevails, and returns home triumphant. (Think of the original Star Wars trilogy with Luke Skywalker battling the "dark side" and celebrating victory with Han Solo, Princess Leia, and the Wookies in the victorious final scene.)

Stories that have this A–Z arc take people for a satisfying emotional roller-coaster ride. Without a beginning, middle, and end, our communication becomes a muddle that makes no sense. The good news is, it doesn't take long to tell a Hero's Journey story. You can do it in a minute or less. In fact, the best NFL Super Bowl commercial of all time, in my opinion, does just that.

The ad shows an exhausted, mud-covered "Mean Joe" Greene limping down the tunnel after a football game. An innocent-faced boy calls his name. "Mean Joe" looks at him, glowering. The boy offers his bottle of Coca-Cola. Joe pauses, takes it, glugs it down, and then starts walking back to the locker room. Dejected, the boy begins to leave.

Suddenly, Joe turns back, says, "Hey, kid," and throws his jersey to him. The kid brightens in wonderment and says a heartfelt "Gee, thanks" while "Mean Joe" flashes a huge smile.

A recent example of a Hero's Journey that has captured the attention of millions is Randy Pausch, who became an instant celebrity after giving a lecture at Carnegie Mellon University, where he was a professor of computer science. As he spoke, he was in the final stages of incurable pancreatic cancer. The videotaped lecture spread like wildfire on YouTube, and then spawned a bestselling book. Why? I think it's because Pausch spoke from the heart about what mattered most to him: about the legacy he wanted to leave.

Does your POP! communication take people on an emotional ride? Do you dare to dig deep and share honestly about what matters to you? Do you *teach* (appeal to intelligence) as well as *touch* (appeal to emotions)? Everyone yearns for from-the-heart-not-just-the-head communication. That's when we truly connect.

HOW TO USE FIRST-PERSON STORIES

If there is magic in storytelling, and I'm convinced there is,
the formula seems to lie solely in the aching urge of the writer
to convey something he feels important to the reader.
JOHN STEINBECK

Step 1. Bring out your W9 Form. What is your priority project? What are you trying to achieve? What is a story you can share where you were challenged by this issue and somehow learned how to overcome it? Put yourself back in those circumstances and write down everything you said, thought, and felt while going through that experience.

Step 2. Interview employees, customers, family members, friends, and other people to find meaningful before-and-after anecdotes that illustrate how they had difficulty with a situation and successfully resolved it because they used your product, idea, or service. Be sure to capture exactly what they were saying or thinking while working through this.

Step 3. What is the origin of your idea or invention? Go back to when you first knew you had to bring this product or process to market. Relive those circumstances and make them come alive so your audience will feel your passion and conviction. Share enough sensory detail so anyone reading or hearing this will be able to visualize what happened.

20

Put People in the Pool

The more specific you are, the more universal you are.
Nancy Hale

Mariah Burton Nelson, one of the country's experts on women in sports, and now Executive Director of the American Society for Physical Activity and Recreation, can frequently be found on ESPN talking about Title IX or other sports issues. She is often hired by corporations and associations to speak to their employees and members on her signature message, "We Are All Athletes."

Mariah starts her keynote by sharing the event that shaped her athleticism and her belief that competition is healthy. Her mother was a fit woman who encouraged Mariah to try many different sports. One summer day while at the pool, her mother challenged five-year-old Mariah to a race. At that point, Mariah pulls the audience into the story and puts them in the pool with her.

You're with her, crouched down on the edge of the pool, toes gripping the edge, leaning slightly forward with her arms behind, ready to throw herself into a flat dive so she can quickly resurface. You're with her as she tenses herself through, "Ready, set," and launches herself the instant her mom yells, "Go!" You're thrashing along with her as she swims as fast as she can, neck and neck with her mom. You imagine her out-of-breath determination, her resolve to finish first. You *stretch* with her last stroke to the edge of the pool, only to be "touched out" by her mom who gets there a fraction of a second earlier. You're there when Mariah comes up, panting for air, and her mom, grinning from ear to ear, slaps the side of the pool triumphantly and says, "Beat ya!"

Did poor little Mariah wilt in defeat, her fragile self-esteem ruined? No. Her mom's healthy approach to doing your best, no matter what, motivated her to work harder so she could win next time. Mariah then segues into how many youth sports leagues these days maintain a "let's not keep score so no one has to be a loser" approach. This leads to her premise that healthy competition is not bad as it challenges people to aspire to excellence.

What's the point? If Mariah simply got onstage and said, "Competition is good for you. It motivates you to do and be your best," people would nod off. Because of her "put 'em in the pool" story, people send her e-mails years later, repeating her "Beat ya" story almost word for word, and sharing how it changed their perception about the value of competition—for the better.

Do you remember the catchphrase technique we discussed earlier about how effective it is to "take the words right out of people's mouths and minds?" When we feature first-person stories with vivid details, people aren't just hearing our words, they're picturing that scene and immersing themselves in the story as if it were happening right now. When you add two-person dialogue and tell both sides of a story, your listeners might as well be sitting in the room with the two of you, watching the conversation take place.

Interestingly, this works with speaking *and* writing. Why is it that we can read a novel for hours at a time and not feel like it's work? Because it has a story with a beginning, middle, and end that features multiperson dialogue. The back-and-forth conversation pulls us into the experience it as if it's happening to us. All of a sudden these are no longer typed words on a piece of paper. We are swept up in this romance, on the edge of our seats with this thriller, turning pages as fast as we can to solve a mystery.

You may have noticed I've used a lot of quotes from writers in this book. That's because we're all writers. Writers aren't just people who author books, articles, promotional material, or web copy. We write (in our minds, on the page, or on the screen) every time we communicate. The words we choose and the way we choose to use them determine whether our communication is successful.

DON'T TELL THE STORY, REENACT IT

Good writing is supposed to evoke sensation in the reader—not the fact that it is raining, but the feeling of being rained upon.
E. L. DOCTOROW

Are you a sales manager? Do you have a staff meeting in the near future? Were you going to pump up your team with exhortations, statistics, and progress reports regarding quotas? Are you supporting any of your points with an example pulled from the field? Could you re-create a closing sale between one of your employees and a customer to demonstrate a point? Can you share a success story, word for word, of one of your staff members? If you do, watch what happens in the room when you reenact that story. It will be so quiet you can hear the proverbial pin drop.

PULL PEOPLE INTO YOUR WORLD

As a reader, I want a book to kidnap me into its world.
ERICA JONG

Does your organization conduct training programs on customer service? Does the instructor simply talk about the importance of making every customer a repeat customer, and give a series of steps on how to achieve that? That can come across as a lecture. Longtime employees may feel their intelligence and experience are being insulted.

A better approach might be to divide the group into triads and give participants fifteen minutes to share an example of:

- a delightful or disastrous customer experience they had elsewhere
- a difficult customer they were able to turn around
- a favorite story about a customer who gave them a meaningful compliment

Watch what happens to the mood of the room when you give people opportunities to share their own personal stories of good and bad service. All of a sudden, the rhetoric becomes real. Depending on the size of the group, you might want to ask each triad to choose one member to "report out" his or her story.

Ask the participants to relive what happened so the rest of the group is on the phone, in the department store, at that restaurant, or on that plane when this was taking place. Ask them to repeat the dialogue verbatim so participants are in the scene as if it were happening to them. Ask the group to pinpoint the factors that made the customer experience positive or negative. Write those customer-service criteria on a poster pad or overhead transparency so the entire group can see them. Notice the group has generated these insights from their own experience.

Ask the group how they can duplicate the good service that happened with that help desk, check-in counter, or store within your organization. Ask for their ideas on how they could prevent or resolve the negative experiences they had with another company.

Ask them to think of specific situations where they don't know what to say or do. Write down exactly what customers say when they're upset. What is an accusation that leaves them tongue-tied? Ask employees to contribute exact phrasing they've learned to use that keeps customers happy, returning, and referring their friends. This participative approach that focuses on real-life experiences rather than generalized theory is much more likely to engage employees and offer meaningful on-the-job improvement.

DON'T TELL, SHOW

*Knowing is not enough, we must apply. Willing is
not enough, we must do.*
JOHANN WOLFGANG VON GOETHE

Dinny Trinidad, human resource director for the Prince Hotel in Waikiki, Hawaii, told me this approach turned their new-hire orientations into something employees looked forward to rather than dreaded. "We used to just cover all the required material (benefit plans, sick leave, CPR, dress policies, etc.), ask new hires if they understood, hand them an employee manual, and send them on their way.

"Now we demonstrate every important point with a real-life example. Instead of just telling about the time one of our bellmen went above and beyond to help a businessman retrieve a briefcase he had left in a cab, we bring in the bellman and let him tell the story. Instead of just talking about a honeymoon couple who returns every year for their anniversary because our front desk manager recognized them and called them by name, we invite that manager to tell how it makes her day when this couple walks in and she welcomes them back.

"By showing good service examples pulled right out of our workplace to make our points, our new hires aren't just flooded with facts; they know exactly what to say and what not to say. They're much more likely to follow these examples because they have 'experienced' them instead of just being told about them. Furthermore, it showcases our seasoned employees and gives them the recognition and 'stardom' they deserve."

HOW TO PUT PEOPLE IN THE POOL

It's gotten to the point where it's not about the technology, it's about storytelling.
STEVE STANFORD

Whether you're writing copy for your blog or delivering a talk to your industry association, you're not finished until you've shared a story with human interaction. When is your next professional communication? Use these steps to make your message even more meaningful by incorporating "pulled from the workplace" dialogue that everyone can relate to and replicate.

Step 1. Identify a story that shares an epiphany that is relevant to your audience and congruent with the purpose of your communication.

Step 2. Who are the "players"? Identify two people who were involved in this situation. Describe them and the scene so readers or listeners can see them in their minds.

Step 3. Chart out what each individual actually said. Capture the exact words and the underlying emotion that was present at the time. Don't tell the story as if it happened a long time ago. Bring it into the present moment by reliving and acting out the scene so your target audience is right there with you in the pool.

21

Craft a Memorable
Money Phrase

You'll get nothing and like it!
TED KNIGHT IN *CADDYSHACK*

Did you see the movie *Jerry Maguire*? If so, you probably remember Cuba Gooding Jr. and Tom Cruise yelling "Show me the money!" at each other over the phone. Within days, millions of people across the country were repeating that phrase.

What other movie one-liners do you remember? Jack Nicholson's "You can't handle the truth" in *A Few Good Men*? Clint Eastwood snarling, "Make my day"? Arnold Schwarzenegger's "I'll be back" in *The Terminator*? The famous "Here's looking at you, kid" from *Casablanca*?

Hollywood producers know that when audience members repeat a key phrase from a movie, it creates a much-welcomed word-of-mouth buzz. That's the power of coming up with a money phrase; it literally and figuratively puts profits in your pocket because it gets remembered and repeated, which means more people are aware of your product, which means more people are interested in trying it or buying it.

In business communication, a "take-away" is what your audience "got" from your message. Did colleagues take away the commitment to think twice before sending an angry e-mail? Did employees take away specific techniques they can use to operate a cash register more effectively? Did prospective customers take away the motivation to buy your brand instead of the one they're currently using?

It doesn't matter whether you talk for one minute, one hour, or one day. At the end of that time, your audience will hopefully have at least one take-away. If they don't, that time was wasted for both of you. If they do leave with a take-away, the next question to ask is, Was it the right take-away? Is what they got what you wanted them to get?

If what they got out of your message is not what you intended, then your intended take-away needs to be highlighted more effectively. The goal is to showcase it so clearly, concisely, and compellingly that it POP!s out of everything you say.

This is much too important to be left to chance. Every time you compose a communication, whether it's copy for your internal newsletter, a welcome speech for a breakfast meeting, or a bid proposal to win a government contract, ask yourself, What is my purpose? What do I want people to do when they walk out of the room, finish this article, or visit my website. What is the precise take-away I want participants to have? What is one specific idea, phrase, action, or decision I want them to leave with and act on?

MONEY PHRASES DRIVE
WORD-OF-MOUTH MARKETING

Where did we go right?!
MONEY PHRASE FROM THE MOVIE *THE PRODUCERS*

Management guru Peter Drucker has said, "There are two functions, and two functions only, of any business: innovation and marketing."

The good news is the POP! process can help you accomplish

both purposes of business. It helps you create innovate messages that market your offering. From now on, look at your e-mails, letters, presentations, training programs, marketing portfolios, staff meetings, internal newsletters, and business websites, and ask yourself, Is this innovative and will it succeed in marketing us so people want to hire us, buy us, or do business with us?

Once you've clarified the primary point you want to make, drive it home with a crafted sound bite. Don't be subtle. Don't bury it. Don't infer it. Don't hope people will somehow intuit what you want them to do. Take responsibility for crafting a money phrase that will deliver the results you want.

IS YOUR AUDIENCE GIVING YOU YOUR SOUND BITE?

Half the world is composed of people who have something
to say and can't, and the other half who have nothing
to say but keep on saying it.

ROBERT FROST

A primary purpose of POP! is to help people learn how to compose what they have to say into a message people actually want to listen to. Interestingly enough, one of the easiest ways to do this is to listen to what they tell you, and then tell it back to them.

John Alston, one of only 125 people in the world to be selected to the National Speakers Association Hall of Fame, delivered a keynote at our national convention that featured one of the most powerful sound bites I've ever heard. As a professional speaker for more than two decades, I've seen hundreds of presentations, yet I remember John's message as if I heard it this morning.

His message was that it's naive to simply hope our children will develop into good citizens on their own. We must take responsibility for modeling integrity and instilling values instead of leaving that to chance. Toward the end of his talk, John threw his arms wide open and thundered, "Goodness must be taught!" The crowd roared, rose as one, and gave him a standing ovation. I still get chicken skin (Hawaiian colloquialism for *goose bumps*) just thinking about it.

I ran into John months later and he mentioned he was writing a book. Glad to hear he was sharing his message on the stage *and* page, I asked, "What's the title?"

I don't even remember what he told me, but it didn't do justice to the power of his message. I couldn't help myself. I asked, "John, why aren't you naming your book *Goodness Must Be Taught!*? I still remember that signature line from your keynote, and that's extremely rare." John agreed that was what audiences seemed to remember and he subsequently named his book *Goodness Must Be Taught!*

Think about it. Have you attended a conference recently? Can you repeat, word for word, *any* ideas you heard from any of those presentations? Probably not, and that's the norm.

If you create a phrase that resonates with everyone who hears it, that phrase has the potential to become your signature line. If you write a one-liner that jumps out of the article, it makes sense to highlight that and maybe even turn it into the headline.

TURN YOUR MONEY PHRASE INTO REVENUE-PRODUCING MERCHANDISE

Are you getting the biggest bang for your brand?
SAM HORN

If you test-market your money phrase and it receives a universally positive reaction, consider turning it into a name brand with merchandise you can sell or give away.

Put your money phrase on your business cards, display it on your website, include it on your letterhead and marketing materials, feature it on your opening and closing PowerPoint slides. You might even think about putting it on coffee mugs, calendars, pens, refrigerator magnets, and other giveaways. The more widely you disseminate and merchandise your money phrase, the more buzz you'll build for your message and the more brand recognition people will have of your concept or creation.

HOW TO CRAFT A MEMORABLE MONEY PHRASE

I always bear the reader in mind, and try to visualize him and watch for any signs of boredom or impatience to flit across his face.
Kingsley Amis

What's a pitch you're preparing? Are you requesting venture capital? Introducing yourself at a network function? Instead of going on and on and on, sum up your point in a Purposeful, Original, Pithy sound bite. Use the following steps to create what my client and colleague Doug Stevenson calls a "phrase that pays."

Step 1. Please bring out your W9 Form. What is *one thing* you want your target audience to remember and do as a result of your communication? Do you want them to order a minimum of one thousand units, vote for your candidate on Election Day, hire you for this job by Monday, switch their account to your bank today?

Step 2. The more specific you are about what action you want people to take, the more likely it is to happen. Craft your money phrase into a clear, concise, and compelling sound bite, using the techniques in Section III. Experiment with alliteration, rhythm, rhymes, and synonyms until you have a phrase that feels right.

Step **3.** Review your material. Is there a story that always elicits a visceral reaction from your audience? Is there a moral to that story that everyone relates to? Condense that into one pithy statement that people instantly get and want.

Step **4.** If nothing is POP!ing for you, take a break. As Stuart Wilde said, "Life was never meant to be a struggle; just a gentle progression from one point to another, much like walking through a valley on a sunny day."

Creativity can be facilitated, not forced. Get outside and go for a walk. The right-left movement of your arms and legs will activate and align both sides of your brain and give you a chance to look at things from a fresh perspective. This can synthesize and distill your swirl of thoughts into an epiphany that produces the perfect money phrase.

Step **5.** Test-market your money phrase by running it by colleagues and customers and reading their reactions. Does it pass the Eyebrow Test? If so, kudos. If not, back to the drafting table. Keep honing it until the majority of people can remember it and repeat it, and are inspired to take the desired action as a result of hearing or seeing your pitch, presentation, or proposal.

22

Make It Relevant with Segues

*A task, which I am trying to achieve, is, by the power of
the written word, to make you hear, to make you
feel—it is before all, to make you see.*
JOSEPH CONRAD

An Olympic athlete was the featured speaker at a business luncheon I recently attended. He had a polished platform presence
and had obviously had a lot of experience telling his story of overcoming injuries, enduring personal sacrifice, and winning despite
questionable judging.

It was interesting, but it consisted primarily of, "then I did this,
then I did that." Never once did he ask the audience if they had experienced something similar. Never once did he extract a lesson
learned and suggest how listeners might benefit from trying this. He
told the group to "go for the gold" and "be all we could be." (Perhaps he was channeling the Army's slogan.) What he didn't do was
make his story our story. As a result, I don't think he was nearly as
effective or inspiring as he could have been.

Our goal, whether it's through the written or spoken word, is to
engage people so thoroughly that they see what we're saying and experience what we experienced so our story becomes their story. As explained in previous chapters, one way to do this is to tell a story with
vibrant detail and human interaction that fully engages their senses.

Another way to do this is to set up segues. Segues occur when we wrap up a story and turn it back to the audience and ask what *they* think. Segues are transitions from our point of view to the customer's. It's when we paint a scenario and then ask our target audience if they've been in that situation. What did they learn?

ESTABLISH TWO-WAY COMMUNICATION

There are two kinds of people in the world—those who walk into
a room and say, "There you are," and those who say, "Here I am."
ABIGAIL VAN BUREN

Sharing only *our* story—"Then I did this, then I said this"—can be off-putting unless we turn it around and ask our audience how this might be true in their lives. Talking or writing only about what happened to us can be indulgent, unless we ask listeners, readers, and viewers how they might be able to benefit from it or apply it.

AT&T's slogan used to be "It's the next best thing to being there." That's exactly what we want to do for our audience. We want to tell our stories so vividly, it's the next best thing to being there. We want them to be imagining this as if it were happening to them. In what way are they experiencing something similar in their job? How can our insight save them some time-consuming trial-and-terror learning? How can they vicariously experience this and take away the epiphany without having to go through the pain?

One way to make *our* story *their* story is to follow examples with "you" questions that cause our audience to reflect upon what we just said and relate it to their circumstances. This "ask, don't tell" approach is called the Socratic Method because Socrates believed the most effective way to teach is to pose questions so students learn through self-discovery. Lecturing is one-way communication.

The teachers are active but their students are passive. Students may hear what's being said, but they may not be assimilating it because they're not fully engaged. Open-ended questions move listeners from an apathetic state to an active state. Now, they're owning the learning process because it's being done *by* instead of *to* them.

HOW TO USE SEGUES

The important thing is not to stop questioning.
ALBERT EINSTEIN

Please look at your message again. Are you sharing a story with human interaction so people are seeing what you're saying? Are you also extracting a lesson learned and asking your audience how this might be relevant or useful for them? Use the steps below to involve your audience so they are fully engaged and applying your insights to their circumstances. If you do, people will buy into what you're saying, or at least take it on board. You're turning your message into a dialogue instead of a monologue.

Step 1. Review your message. What are your major points? Do you wrap up each point by transitioning back to your audience with "you" questions such as:

- Has a customer ever said something like this to you? How did you respond?
- Are your employees multitasking and rushing from one project to the next?
- Have you ever faced this as a manager? How did you handle it?
- Do you have a mentor to turn to when you need advice?

- Would you like to be able to delegate that responsibility and get it off your desk?
- Does it seem people only notice what you do wrong, never what you do right?
- Is your company going through a major change like this?

Step 2. Craft a variety of "you" questions so no matter who is in the audience, they can identify with what you're saying. Develop a demographically balanced mix of questions so no one feels left out. The goal is to have people nodding in recognition because what you're saying is pulled right out of their daily circumstances.

Step 3. How are you making your story their story? Compose several "Have you ever experienced this?", "Does this sound familiar?", "Where is this happening for you?" questions so audience members are applying your insight to a previous, current, or future situation in their lives.

23

Juxtapose Points to Make Them Crystal Clear

*I would go without shirt or shoe . . . sooner than lose for
a minute the two separate sides of my head.*

RUDYARD KIPLING

Hopefully, by now, you agree that the POP! process is both an art
and a science.

It is an art because it is a right-brain process that helps us make
quantum creative leaps and crystallize something that didn't exist
moments before. POP! Art messages have the power to capture our
imaginations, delight our senses, stir our souls, and move us to act.

The POP! process is also a science because it is a step-by-step
system. It doesn't rely solely on chance, luck, or whimsy. It is a left-
brain methodology anyone can replicate. It uses the scientific
method of trial and error to solve a problem. The problem is the decision makers who control the destiny of our concept or creation are
busy, maybe even resistant. We need to craft messages that break
through their preoccupation or objections and win their buy-in.
Like scientists, we experiment with different techniques, eliminating
what doesn't work, until we come up with a solution that achieves
our desired purpose: a Purposeful, Original, Pithy Tell 'n Sell message that captures and keeps their favorable interest.

The POP! process is also an art and a science because we use both sides of our head (the factual left brain and the feeling right brain) to compose and craft our communication so it is practical and persuasive. We want to engage our audience's heads and hearts so they are engaged both intellectually and emotionally. An easy and direct way to do this is to juxtapose your points in left and right columns.

What is juxtaposition? It's a technique by which you place words, phrases, or concepts side by side to provide contrast or comparison.

DEPICT YOUR POINTS SIDE BY SIDE

Much of my writing is verbal painting.
ELIZABETH BOWEN

Juxtaposing your points, or verbally painting them, as Elizabeth Bowen says so eloquently, presents information in a way that takes rhetoric out of the conceptual and makes it visual so people can eyeball it and understand it.

This approach doesn't just help your audience quickly grasp complex points, but it also helps make them proprietary. Remember earlier in the book we talked about how we're one of many? We're one of many psychologists talking about how to be a better parent. We're one of many financial experts trying to persuade people to eliminate credit card debt. We're one of many Realtors trying to convince home-buyers to work with us.

If we just talk, talk, talk about our offering, we'll sound like everyone else. Even if we have innovative suggestions or viable, valuable services, they'll get lost in the sheer outpouring of words.

To prevent our message from being quickly forgotten, divide it into a dual construct. The construct is initially arbitrary. In the beginning, you're making this up. You're not basing this on anyone else's work. You are developing your own intellectual property.

Get a fresh piece of paper and divide it into two columns, selecting one of the following constructs to summarize the dos and dont's of your message or the pros and cons of your product, proposal, or process.

Wrong	Right
Before	After
Curse	Blessing
In the past	In the future
What hurts communication	What helps communication
What sabotages success	What supports success
What compromises performance	What contributes to performance
What breaks a relationship	What builds a relationship
What prevents sales	What produces sales

By now, you've seen a trend. When possible, make the two contrasting approaches alliterative. And no, to answer your question, your matching concepts don't have to start with the same sound, but alliteration does show a level of craftsmanship most people will appreciate and it increases the likelihood your language will be singular. The more precise your words, the more powerful your communication. There could be hundreds of professionals addressing this topic, or offering a similar service or product, but *no one* will have your unique approach.

Comparisons can help customers and employees see the before and after of a concept more clearly. It reduces an overwhelming "I can't remember all that" volume of information into a concise "I get it now" visual format. It is a way to extract and visually present the crucial points of your message. Instead of trying to get across everything you know about this subject, you get across the essence of what's most important.

Juxtaposing also lends itself to licensing and merchandising.

Visually contrasting components of your offering can Cliff Note your take-away points, your product's benefits, or your methodology's steps in an easy-to-grasp format. It's obvious these words weren't just thrown together haphazardly or spontaneously. You invested time and brainpower to purposely develop and position these words to have maximum value.

Put your juxtaposed phrases on bookmarks, refrigerators magnets, and posters that can be placed in offices. Now your message is getting out to even more people, all because you took the time to design your message in a visual style that gives it Idea Equity.

MORE IS NOT BETTER

There is a time to say nothing, and a time to say something,
but there is never a time to say everything.
·Anonymous

Imagine you are a trainer developing a course on how employees can improve their communication. You might want to break this huge topic into something "graspable" by introducing the concept that there are "fighting phrases" and "friendly phrases."

You could point out that every time we communicate, we either create conflict or collaboration. Fighting phrases such as *but, should, you'll have to, can't because* create resentment. Friendly phrases such as *and, next time, could you please, yes, as soon as* create rapport.

Now, look again at the above paragraph. It may make sense, but it's hard to grasp what was said. You would probably just move on to the next paragraph and never get the full value of those ideas because they weren't presented in a diagram that helped you picture them in your mind.

Now, imagine if you graphically depicted that information by placing the "wrong" and the "right" types of communication in separate columns, as below.

Fighting Phrases	Friendly Phrases
But	And
Should	Next time
You'll have to	Could you please
Can't because	Yes, you can, as soon as
There's nothing	There's something

JUXTAPOSITION VISUALLY ORGANIZES IDEAS

*Organization is what you do before you do it, so when
you do it, it's not all messed up.*
WINNIE THE POOH

The above construct doesn't tell the "whole story"; it simply provides employees with a succinct, visually organized summary of what they learned. In the program itself, you would tell stories with human interaction that show (rather than tell) how these phrases either hurt or help relationships.

At the end of the course, you could distribute a reminder card with juxtaposed points on it and ask participants, "Have you heard of OOS-OOM?" That may get a "Huh?" Then ask, "Have you ever been to a workshop, and when you leave you're all fired up and raring to go, and then two weeks later everything's back to normal?"

Participants would probably nod and agree they've been there, done that. Then you could let them know that OOS-OOM stands for *Out of Sight, Out of Mind.* To make sure they continue to apply what they've learned, suggest they keep their reminder card *In Sight, In Mind,* where they'll see it frequently throughout the day. By putting it on or near their computer, desk, employee bulletin board, or lunchroom refrigerator, they will be reminded of (and more likely to apply) these crucial points on an ongoing basis.

If you use this idea within your organization, ask your company to pay for these reminder cards to be manufactured, distributed, and posted. If you are an entrepreneur, you might want to produce these cards in bulk as a profit center. Sell them at the back of the room at your programs, trade shows, industry events, and on your website. You can also give them as bonus gifts to meeting planners, prospective clients, and conference participants. You might even magnetize your reminder cards so they're easy to affix.

HOW TO USE JUXTAPOSITION

Every time you open your mouth to talk, your mind
walks out and parades up and down the words.
EDWIN H. STUART

From now on, before you open your mouth to talk, put pen to paper, or place fingers on the keys, use these steps to make sure your parade of words POP!s out and stays in.

Step 1. Review your message. What aspect of your information lends itself to a "before and after" scenario? Where can you point out the wrong way and the right way to perform a task, interact with an employee, or treat a customer?

Step 2. Draw a line down the center of a fresh piece of paper. Put *Don't* on the top of the left column and *Do* on the top of the right column.

Step 3. Start listing in the left-hand column what people don't want to do regarding your topic. What are the behaviors that would sabotage their success, the words that would hurt their relationships, the beliefs that would undermine their effectiveness?

Step 4. Start listing in the right-hand column what people do want to do regarding your topic. What are the behaviors that would support their success, the words that would help their relationships, the beliefs that would add to their effectiveness?

Step 5. Place associated dos and don'ts opposite each other so people can eyeball your visually organized chart and instantly grasp what is hurtful, what is helpful. To the degree possible and appropriate, craft corresponding recommendations so they're alliterative. Get out your thesaurus and look up synonyms for the words until you make meaningful matches. Don't force it. The primary goal is for this to be crystal clear so it's easy to grasp and remember.

Step 6. Create a tangible product featuring your juxtaposed intellectual capital and your money phrase so your audience can continue to benefit from it and you can continue to profit from it. Place your crafted sound bites on reminder cards, on postcards, on the back of your business card, throughout your website and marketing materials, and on merchandise you can sell and give away so you're branding yourself in your audience's minds in a mutually beneficial way.

24

Open Eyes, Ears, Hearts, and Minds with Aha! Quotes

I quote others only the better to express myself.
MONTAIGNE

I guess you can tell I like quotes.

My first public presentation was for my eighth-grade graduation. Being selected class valedictorian was a big deal for me and I spent hours preparing.

A week before the big day, I asked my father to critique my eight-minute talk. Dad was Director of Vocational Agriculture Education for the State of California, which included overseeing the Future Farmers of America program. FFA is committed to developing students' speaking skills because it believes the ability to speak clearly, confidently, and convincingly is as important to professional success as talent and hard work. Dad had judged many speaking competitions on the state and national levels, and was an impressive public speaker who learned how to be comfortable in front of a group from his father, who was the president of Toastmasters International in 1951.

Dad patiently listened to my "bird ready to leave the nest and fly on its own" homily. When I finished, he was silent for a moment. Then, knowing I wanted honest feedback, he said simply, "It's a good enough talk, but it's similar to other commencement speeches

I've heard." He continued, "Sam, if you're going to ask people for their valuable time and attention, it is your responsibility to say something original."

I protested, "But, Dad, there's nothing new under the sun."

He smiled and said, "Sure there is. Want to know what the definition of *original* is? If we haven't heard it before, it's original."

People are delighted when we introduce new ideas that make them laugh out loud, reflect, and reconsider what they thought they knew to be true. That's one of the many benefits of using a thought-provoking quote. If your audience hasn't seen or heard it before, it's original to them. They feel enlightened because they now know something they didn't know a minute before.

MAKE THE TRIED AND TRUE . . . NEW

As Spinoza, or someone very much like him, once said . . .
JUDITH VIORST

To make your quotations maximally effective on the page and stage, follow these tips:

Tip #1. Steer clear of common quotes. They defeat the whole purpose. If you've heard it before, your audience has heard it before. If the quote is perfect for your purposes, then neutralize your audience's anticipated objections with this disclaimer: "I imagine many of you are already familiar with this popular quote. I chose to use it anyway because . . ." Then briefly explain why you feel this saying is particularly meaningful or insightful.

Tip #2. Be demographically correct. Appeal to a diverse audience by keeping a gender, ethnic, age, and industry balance in your quote sources. Any extreme will become noticeable and potentially offensive. If you quote only men, only Caucasians, or tell one sports story after another, that could become a turnoff to some of your listeners or readers.

Tip #3. Feature a variety of classic and current sources. Make your work timeless and contemporary at the same time by quoting everyone from Aristotle to ZZ Top. By tapping into the wisdom of our elders, you ensure that your work will stand the test of time. By tapping into observations from leaders in today's headlines, you ensure your material is topical.

Tip #4. Quote sources respected by your target audience. I'll never forget the time I quoted Jane Fonda in a workshop for the U.S. Navy. Not a good idea. Jane, of course, was famous for protesting the Vietnam War, and these military officers did not appreciate the fact that I was using her as an example. Learn from my mistake and do your homework so anyone you hold up as an example meets your customers' approval.

Tip #5. Be funny and philosophical. Make 'em laugh; make 'em think. Adding humor makes people like you; adding insights makes people learn from you. Featuring laugh-out-loud quotes along with thought-provoking quotes gives people an emotional roller-coaster experience. A favorite is Henny Youngman, who said, "I told my doctor I broke my leg in two places. He said, 'Stop going to those places.'" You could then segue into your point about "Are we repeating behavior that isn't working?"

Tip #6. Always attribute. It's okay to riff off other people's insights (as long as we give credit where credit is due); it's not okay to *rip* off people's insights.

Tip #7. Deliver quotes without notes. When done well, a quote with your variation on it makes a magnificent money phrase. That means it's worth memorizing and polishing so you can look the audience in the eyes and deliver it for maximum impact. If you're thinking, The quote I want to use is too long to memorize, that quote may be too long to use. Remember, if they can't repeat it, they didn't get it.

IT CAN BE OKAY, EVEN ADVISABLE, TO QUOTE YOURSELF

I like to quote myself to spice up the conversation.
GEORGE BERNARD SHAW

I used to think it was egotistical to quote yourself. I now understand that if you create a money phrase and don't credit yourself, you've just forfeited all the money you deserve to make from that phrase.

I learned this the hard way. Over my twenty-five years (yikes!) as a professional speaker, I've done my best to follow my father's advice. I've felt it was my responsibility to be original, so I've been diligent about creating my own intellectual capital. I've created terminology and crafted many money phrases. But I didn't officially put my name on them. As a result, other entrepreneurs ran with them and turned them into profitable presentations and products.

As my sons would say, "My bad."

So you may notice that I quote myself several times in this book. That's not conceit. I've done that on purpose to model that if *you* create a money phrase, you need to credit yourself for it. In these days of domain names and brand names, you deserve to profit on your intellectual capital. It's naive to think or do otherwise.

COMB THE NEWSPAPERS FOR CURRENT QUOTES

*The wisdom of the wise and the experience of
the ages are perpetuated by quotations.*
BENJAMIN DISRAELI

Will your audience be wiser after hearing or seeing your message? They might be if you include a topical quote from that day's newspaper. The above quote from Disraeli is profound, but if we use quotes solely from philosophers who lived hundreds of years ago, our audience may wonder how current our information is.

As mentioned in the Laugh Line chapter, one way to tap into the day's zeitgeist is to refer humorously to a frustration everyone shares. It's a way of creating a community because people feel they're in on the joke. For example, Sandra Bernhard was on one of the late-night talk shows, and the conversation turned to what a nuisance cell phones had become. One of the other guests mentioned she had caller ID and never answered the phone in public unless it was crucial. The quick-witted Bernhard said, "Yeah, what I'm waiting for is caller IQ."

Quoting a smart, witty zinger like that can make you seem hip instead of ho-hum. That's why scanning a local and national newspaper the morning of a presentation, whether it's to your board of directors, stockholders, or employees at your weekly sales meeting, is one of the best twenty-minute investments you can make.

When you find something that pertains to your issue, cut it out and bring it with you so you can share the pertinent statistic, quote, or paragraph with your group. The fact that you went to the effort to bring in something from that day's paper will indicate your commitment to sharing up-to-date info. Furthermore, it may give you a delightful opportunity to pleasantly surprise your audience with original material, further raising your approval ratings.

That's what happened this fall when I was asked to speak to a group of business leaders. I got up early that morning to read the papers, and my discipline was rewarded by an "almost too good to be true" article in the October 15, 2005, issue of the *Washington Post* titled "California Couple with Empty Nest Gets Serious About Downsizing." The article by Holly Hayes told the story of Steve and Judy Glickman who traded in their 2,300-square-foot, five-bedroom home on a cul-de-sac for a, drum roll, please, *chicken coop*.

The Glickmans' two sons had moved on to college and they realized they were using only 30 percent of their home. So they moved into this 544-square-foot, one-bedroom, one-bath home, said to be the smallest house on the smallest lot in the country. It was originally built as a chicken coop for the house next door. The article reported the Glickmans paid $545,000 for their new home (a result of the hot real estate market in the San Jose–San Francisco area).

Quoting that article definitely got the group's attention and served as an interesting lead-in to a discussion of how teams can adapt to just about anything (my presentation was billed as "Full Team Ahead"). It also gave me a dream opportunity to play off the theme of unintentional miscommunication. I told the audience I could just imagine the Glickmans looking at each other with eyes as big as saucers as Judy told Steve, "No, I said, 'Why don't we *fly* the coop?!'"

That got a big laugh, a segue into how easy it can be to misunderstand teammates, and a return speaking engagement, at least partially because I quoted that article.

QUOTATIONS ARE A QUICK WAY
TO ESTABLISH PRECEDENCE

We should learn from the mistakes of others. We don't
have time to make them all ourselves.

GROUCHO MARX

Think of quotations as "verbal shorthand." They condense complicated concepts into an accessible language nugget. Even more importantly, these pearls of wisdom can inspire people to change their ways because they point out precedence and show how others have already benefited from adopting a constructive behavior or belief. They help people learn from the mistakes *and* the successes of others.

For example, if you're a basketball fan, you may be familiar with the feud between seven-foot-tall Shaquille O'Neal and youthful sharpshooter Kobe Bryant that occurred toward the end of their time together as teammates on the Los Angeles Lakers. Insults were exchanged in person and in the press, and the two notoriously avoided even looking at each other in 2005 when they faced each other on court.

Their very public spat came to an end on January 16, 2006, when O'Neal, now playing for the Miami Heat, approached Bryant during the pregame warm-ups and congratulated him on the birth of his daughter and the upcoming birth of a second child. A few minutes later, the longtime adversaries shook hands and exchanged a few words and a hug at center court before the tip-off.

"It made me feel good," Byrant said in a January 18, 2006, *Washington Post* article, adding that he was surprised at O'Neal's goodwill gesture.

What inspired O'Neal to extend the olive branch? "I had orders from the great Hall of Famer Bill Russell," O'Neal said. "People thought Russell and Wilt Chamberlain hated each other, but Bill told me they spoke once or twice a week before Wilt passed away. Martin Luther King was an ambassador of peace, and it's his birthday today. Bill Russell told me how rivalries should be, and that I should shake Kobe Bryant's hand, let bygones be bygones, and bury the hatchet."

In my mind, O'Neal demonstrated what a "big man" he truly is by initiating that peacemaking gesture. If you are a consultant working with an office staff that's mired in conflict, you could speak about the cost of carrying grudges. Instead of being content to share platitudes about how important it is to get along and forgive and forget, you could hold up that article, read O'Neal's words about his rationale behind his actions, and let his example eloquently make your point for you.

Quoting a respected individual who has successfully done what you're suggesting to your audience is to let that individual do your talking for you. It's a way of saying, "You don't have to take my word on this. Here's proof this is valid and it works."

HOW TO USE AHA! QUOTATIONS

All Shakespeare did was to string together a lot of old,
well-known quotations.
H. L. MENCKEN

What's a situation in which you'll be communicating soon? Follow the above guidelines and use the following steps to make your material more compelling by accessing the wisdom of the ages and more contemporary by accessing a current headline to add topicality.

Step 1. Get out the Core Words you use to explain your concept or project.

Step 2. Go online to your favorite search engine (Google, Yahoo!, Ask.com) and enter the words *quote dictionary*. Select one that looks promising—my favorite is www.thinkexist.com—and then key in your Core Words. This will provide (unless your Core Words are uncommon) dozens of quotations that contain your key words.

Step 3. Don't be content to use familiar quotes. Your criteria ought to be, Does it stop me in my tracks? Does it cause me to laugh, think, or appreciate something new?

Step 4. Be sure your quotations meet the criteria covered in this chapter. Do you have gender balance? Both classic and contemporary sources? Insider experts your target audience knows and respects?

Step 5. Focus on a key word of each quotation and relate it back to your topic so audience members know exactly how this applies to your point. Follow each quotation with a question so people relate it to their situation instead of hearing it without context.

25

Inspire Action with Specific Next Steps

Action may not always bring happiness,
but there is no happiness without action.
BENJAMIN DISRAELI

The premise of this book is that it is *our* responsibility to craft pitches, titles, and taglines that capture and keep our customers' interest. If customers aren't paying attention, if audience members aren't listening, if decision makers aren't buying, it's our fault—not theirs.

I hope the techniques in this book have helped you design and deliver messages that POP! out and stay in your target audience's minds. This last chapter offers one more technique to motivate them to act on your message so they start, stop, or do something differently as a result of your communication.

As POP! communicators our goal is *not* just to have people think, "Wow, what a funny ad," or "What a clever title," or "What a well-designed site." POP! has an ulterior motive.

Our goal is to (1) get people's attention and (2) motivate them to take a certain action—whether that is to vote for our candidate, fund our start-up, buy our product, hire our company, attend our movie, or read our book.

It's our job to switch people from *thinking* about what they've heard or read to *acting* on what they've just heard or read.

The good news is there's an easy way to prompt people to act. Simply use the words *next time*. As in, "What are you going to do next time _____?" Then fill in the blank. The next time you have a cold? The next time you need a branding consultant? The next time you want to buy a car?

You can also use the words *from now on*. As in, From now on, what will you say if . . .

- a member tells you she's not going to rejoin the association?
- a venture capitalist says no to your proposal?
- a hotel tells you the price for your business breakfast has doubled?
- a valued employee is going through a difficult divorce?

Another phrase that can inspire people to follow up and take action is *in the future*. As in, In the future, if _____, what will you say or do? For example, What would you say or do in the future if . . .

- a consulting client keeps asking for favors and free advice?
- an angry guest says, "You don't care about your customers!"
- a colleague says something that borders on sexual harassment?
- a coworker wants to talk but you're too busy?

RECIPES DON'T MAKE COOKIES

You don't save a pitcher for tomorrow. Tomorrow it may rain.
BASEBALL COACH LEO DUROCHER

Chapter 24 explained how quotations can be used to make your message elicit an "aha." Profound quotes not only provoke thought, but they can also can provoke change. If you want to motivate people to get out of complacency and into motion, you might want to share one of the following sayings and give the group time to clarify exactly what they're going to do starting now, not someday.

- "Let us then, be up and doing."—Longfellow
- "The future starts today, not tomorrow."—Pope John Paul II
- "Success often comes to those who dare and act; it seldom goes to the timid who are ever afraid of consequences." —Jawaharlal Nehru
- "Let us always be open to the miracle of the second chance." —David Stier
- "Action is the antidote to despair."—Joan Baez

UPDATE YOUR MESSAGE

The mark of a successful organization isn't whether or not it has problems; it's whether it has the same problems it had last year.
JOHN FOSTER DULLES

As Dulles pointed out, successful organizations adapt to changing circumstances. POP! messages also need to be adapted to changing circumstances. A purpose that existed for our product last year may no longer be current. That's why it's important to revisit the W Questions in Section II every year and update your W9 Form. Chances are, you'll get different answers because your circumstances are different. And if your circumstances are different, your POP! message needs to reflect that difference.

An excellent example of an organization that updated and adapted its mission is the 117-year-old Tournament of Roses Association. The Rose Parade, traditionally held on January 1 in Pasadena,

California, draws thousands of fans who line Colorado Boulevard to ooh and aah over the marching bands and flower-bedecked floats. In 2006, the governing committee realized its primary purpose had changed from pleasing the thousands along the parade route to pleasing the fifty million people from around the world who watched on TV. It added pizzazz for TV viewers by starting the event with singers, dancers, and aerial performers and by stopping the parade at midpoint for an extravaganza featuring Toni Braxton and magician Lance Burton.

Tournament of Roses President Libby Evans Wright explained the new focus by saying, "When you're looking at yourself as a brand or a product or a business, you always want to keep renewing yourself. You want to keep yourself vibrant and interesting to your market. We've made these additions based on market research that found our television viewers wanted more entertainment."

What do your customers want more of? What will motivate them to "stay tuned"? Does your marketing campaign address their current interests and present-day circumstances?

A recent ad campaign demonstrates the power of tapping into the public's zeitgeist. Parents often griped about their kids being obsessed with their Game Boys during family vacations. The roles today are reversed with kids complaining that their folks ignore them while tapping away at their laptop or BlackBerry. A brilliant "Visit Orlando" ad addresses this issue by showing a father happily playing in the pool with his son. A sidebar shows this dialogue: *"Daddy, wanna go swimming?" "Yes." "Daddy, can you carry me on your shoulders?" "Yes." "Daddy, will you leave your phone in the room?" "Yes."* The subliminal message? Come to Orlando and have an old-fashioned family vacation where you have fun playing together instead of with your gadgets.

POP! AT ITS BEST

Mend your speech a little lest you mar your fortunes.
WILLIAM SHAKESPEARE

I'm often asked for the "best of the best" examples of POP! messages. I've sprinkled many of my favorites throughout this book, and I've honored the top ten in the POP! Hall of Fame on page 223.

I also believe that POP! can operate on a grander scale. To paraphrase Shakespeare, I think we should mend our speech a little so we can *make* our fortunes.

When you think about it, the individuals in the last few centuries who have made the most impact are the communicators who stirred our minds and souls with their passionately felt eloquence and intent. There have been thousands of leaders, but who do we remember? Martin Luther King's "I have a dream," Franklin Delano Roosevelt's "The only thing we have to fear is fear itself," and John F. Kennedy's "Ask not what your country can do for you."

History is made and remembered in compelling sound bites. As Leo Rosten said, "Those who truly shape our destiny are those who use words with clarity, grandeur, and passion."

USE POP! FOR HIGHER-PURPOSE COMMUNICATION

*Once a human being has arrived on this earth, communication
is the largest single factor determining what kinds of relationships
he makes with others and what happens to him.*

VIRGINIA SATIR

Satir's observation bears serious consideration. If you want to capture and keep people's attention, the techniques in this book can help you do that. If you want to communicate in a way that shapes people's minds and actions, you can also use these techniques for a higher purpose.

Hopefully, we don't just want to be noticed, heard, bought, and remembered. We want to positively influence others through the power of our words.

Chicken Soup for the Writer's Soul coauthor Bud Gardner says, "When you speak, your words echo across the room or down the hall. But when you write, your words echo down the ages." If you invest the brainpower to design and deliver a higher-purpose POP! message, your words can echo across the room, down the hall, and down the ages.

Up until Senator Barack Obama (D–Illinois) took the stage at the 2004 Democratic National Convention, he was a local politician who was well-known and respected in the Chicago community, but not a household name outside his own state. That all changed after his stirring presentation that took the convention and TV audience by storm. His passionate story of his roots and dreams captured people's imaginations, was widely praised by bipartisan reporters, and launched him into the limelight. He was soon swamped with requests to appear on political talk shows and (as I write this) is the 2008 Democratic candidate for president of the United States.

Barack Obama certainly made the most of his fifteen-minute

spotlight. Are you ready to make the most of yours? What you do during your fifteen seconds or fifteen minutes determines whether your impact is a one-time thing or an ongoing thing.

If you capitalize on your window of opportunity by sharing a Purposeful, Original, and Pithy message that is clear, concise, and compelling, people will want more of you. Your moment in the spotlight can be parlayed into a lifelong opportunity to impact others.

When I work with professionals who are preparing presentations or pitches, or who are going to be interviewed by the media, they're often overly focused on the petty stuff, like how they'll look. I tell them their heart is more important than their hair. I tell them to repeat this mantra before they go onstage, on camera, or get in front of the decision makers.

I'm here to serve, not to show off.
I'm here to inform, not to impress.
I'm here to do good, not to look good.
I'm here to make a difference, not a name.

I suggest they repeat this to themselves again and again in the moments before they speak to clarify why we communicate. We don't communicate because we want people to be impressed with our outfit. We communicate because we want to share a message that matters. We communicate because we've learned something, discovered something, or believe we have something to offer that will benefit these people.

If you ground yourself by repeating that mantra, and if you've crafted a message with these techniques, your message will POP! because it's coming from the truest source of eloquence—passionate conviction. If you look into the eyes of your audience, or picture them while writing your message, and genuinely try to reach them with your words, your communication will connect. That is the purpose of language.

HOW TO USE SPECIFIC NEXT STEPS TO INSPIRE ACTION

Once you've done the mental work, there comes a point you have to throw yourself into action and put your heart on the line.
PHIL JACKSON

For a final time in this book I ask, What is a communication you're preparing? Use the following steps to plant the action thought seeds in your decision makers' minds so they are absolutely clear about what you want them to do and are motivated to do it.

Step 1. What is the purpose of your communication? What do you want your target audience to stop, start, or do differently? What do you want decision makers to approve?

Step 2. Someone once asked golfer Ben Hogan, who won the U.S. Open four times, "What's the most important shot in golf?" He smiled and said, "The next one." Have you included a *next time*, a *from now on*, or an *in the future*? Have you included a specific time and date by which they need to act?

Step 3. Have you given them enough time to formulate a follow-up plan? Have you planted specific mental seeds of how they can take action so they don't have to guess what to do or think up something from scratch? Are their action plans feasible?

Step 4. Have you given them an opportunity to write or say what they intend to do? A chance to verbally share their action plan with a colleague or the group? The more senses people use to imprint their follow-up plan, the more likely they are to do it. Writing, saying, and seeing their action plan in print makes it tangible, cements their sense of obligation, and transforms a vague vow into a concrete commitment.

Step 5. This is worth repeating one more time: Review your existing marketing materials annually (if not more often) to make sure they're current. Your pitch, title, and tagline may have been perfect when you created them months (or years) ago. The question is, do they tap into today's zeitgeist?

Agatha Christie said, "Is there ever any particular spot where one can put one's finger and say, 'It all began that day, at such a time and such a place, with such an incident'?"

I love this topic, and I have thoroughly enjoyed writing this book. I hope you've found it interesting and insightful, and that starting today, at this time and this place, you're able to use these techniques to create Purposeful, Original, Pithy messages that help you and your ideas stand out in any crowd so you get more of what you want, need, and deserve.

POP! Hall of Fame

In a Q & A session following a recent keynote, a participant raised his hand and asked me, "Do you, like David Letterman, have a top ten list?"

My first reaction was, "What a great question." I thought about it and came up with these. As you can imagine, the list keeps changing as I run across new pitches, titles, and taglines that impress me with their brilliance. For now, these are my all-time POP! Hall of Famers because they model the power of being Purposeful, Original, and Pithy.

1. *Snuba.* Snorkeling meets scuba in this example, which proves that POP! isn't just about clever wordplay. Coining a proprietary Half-and-Half word has the ability to create a new multimillion-dollar industry.
2. *Weeding by Example.* New Orleans's Jack McShane shows that anyone, even a thirteen-year-old social entrepreneur, can be a creative genius and obtain support for his cause if he invests the time and effort to give his creation a stop-'em-in-their-tracks name.
3. *Yappy Hour.* A Holiday Inn in Virginia received millions of dollars of free media attention and stood out from the crowd by providing a "petworking" alternative to the bark park.

4. *Diabesity.* Dr. Francine Kaufman demonstrated that the best way to corner a niche is to create a niche; and the best way to create a niche is to Cliff Note your concept into a concise sound bite that names a cultural phenomenon.

5. *Freakonomics.* Kudos to authors Steven D. Levitt and Stephen J. Dubner for proving we're all intrigued by seeing things a new way, and for conjuring up a memorable title that has helped their book POP! off the shelves—and has reinvigorated a sleepy corner of academia.

6. *Java Jacket.* Hats off to Jay Sorenson for turning a honeycombed insulating sleeve into a trademarked, alliterative brand—and for turning a generic product into a genius one.

7. *Aflac* and **GEICO.** Congrats for running with ad campaigns that showcase what can happen when you transform a confusing company name into something we can *see*, relate to, and remember.

8. *"E = mcSquirrel"* and *"No beak, no feathers, no service."* These exceedingly clever, stopped-me-in-my-tracks slogans and merchandise for Sky Café ("the Fort Knox of Bird Feeders") actually outsell the original product.

9. *"Great minds like a think"* and *"Good things come to those who walk."* These taglines for the *Economist* and for Avon's walk-a-thons to benefit breast cancer research show that by rearranging clichés instead of repeating them, you can put a fresh twist on a familiar phrase and produce a classy slogan that attracts loyal customers.

10. *Washington Post* and *USA Today.* Thanks for providing attention-grabbing headlines on a daily basis that illustrate how to get anyone interested in anything . . . in seconds.

Index

About the Author

*I have the world's best job. I get paid to hang
out in my imagination all day.*
Stephen King

Sam Horn, the Intrigue Expert, is an award-winning communication/creativity consultant with a twenty-year track record of results speaking for such international clients as the *Fortune* 500 Forum, NASA, the Young Presidents Organization, Hewlett-Packard, Kaiser Permanente, the IRS, the National Governors Association, KPMG, the U.S. Navy, the American Bankers Association, and INC 500.

Sam has helped thousands of entrepreneurs and organizations crystallize compelling brands, book titles, and business names that helped them become the go-to resource in their industry. As John Jantsch (*Fortune*'s number one blogger on small business) said, "Sam is a seriously energetic, creative thinker who has taken what, for some, is mind-boggling work and turned it into a system on how to create memorable names, core marketing messages, and one-of-a-kind slogans."

Sam is the author of six well-reviewed books from major publishers, including *Tongue Fu!*, *What's Holding You Back*, *ConZentrate*, and *Take the Bully by the Horns*. Her books have been translated into seventeen languages (including Chinese, Japanese, Korean, Spanish, French, and German), favorably reviewed in *Publishers Weekly*, the

Chicago Tribune, *Investors Business Daily*, and *Foreign Service Journal*, and endorsed by high-profile individuals ranging from Stephen R. Covey, Rabbi Harold Kushner, and Billie Jean King.

Sam is an in-demand media resource whose work has been featured on every major TV and radio network, including MSNBC, National Public Radio, *Tonight Show with Jay Leno*, and *To Tell The Truth*, where she and her Tongue Fu! team stumped the panel.

Sam is the sixteen-time emcee of the world-renowned Maui Writers Conference and annually coordinates the Nonfiction Retreat the week before the Labor Day weekend conference and at off-site programs in Fiji, Alaska, the Bahamas, and Mexico.

As the originator of the POP! Process and the IDEApreneur Process, she teaches people how to develop commercially viable ideas that make a positive difference for others and a prosperous living for them. She interviews creative thought-leaders in her monthly "Sam's Salon" tele-interviews and holds weekend book camps and speaker camps around the country.

Sam lives on a lake in Reston, Virginia, near Washington, DC's Dulles Airport, where she has the best of both worlds. She can hop on a plane in minutes to keynote a convention, be downtown at the National Press Club in a half hour, or go for a swim in her backyard. Not too shabby. She is the proud mother of two sons, Tom and Andrew, both graduates of Virginia Tech.

SAM WANTS TO HEAR FROM YOU!

Want to arrange for Sam to share these POP! techniques with your association members or employees? Discover for yourself why she was selected as the 2003–04 Outstanding Capital Speaker and why she receives raves for her rollicking presentations that have audiences laughing; thinking, "I didn't know that!"; taking notes; and on their feet cheering.

Want to consult one-on-one with Sam; find out when she'll be speaking in your area; interview her for your publication, TV program, or radio show; or register for one of her weekend camps? Visit www.SamHornPOP.com or call her office at 1 (800) SAM-3455.

Want to see what POP!ed out this week and how you can apply it to your business? Check out Sam's blog at www.SamHornPOP .wordpress.com.

Has a clever headline or tagline caught your attention? Have you created a one-of-a-kind brand, book title, business name, or pitch using the techniques in this book? E-mail it to Sam at Sam@SamHorn.com. With your permission, she'll feature you and your submission in her monthly newsletter. Who knows, you may make her annual POP! Hall of Fame and your priority project will be introduced to millions of new customers.